God's Pottery:
*The Sea of Names &
the Pierced Inheritance*

God's Pottery: *The Sea of Names & the Pierced Inheritance*

© Anne Hamilton 2016
Published by Armour Books
P. O. Box 492, Corinda QLD 4075, Australia
www.armourbooks.com

Cover Photo Credits: Gino Santa Maria (Jesus holding water jar) & justdd (Green Nebula)
Interior design and layout by Book Whispers

ISBN: 978-1-925380-04-0

National Library of Australia Cataloguing-in-Publication entry

Creator: Hamilton, Anne, 1954- author.
Title: God's pottery: the sea of names & the pierced inheritance / Anne Hamilton.

ISBN: 9781925380040 (paperback)

Subjects: Covenant theology.

   Spiritual life--Christianity.

Dewey Number: 231.76

All rights reserved. No part of this publication may be reproduced, stored in, or introduced into a retrieval system, or transmitted, in any form, or by any means (electronic, mechanical, photocopying, recording or otherwise) without the prior written permission of the publisher.

God's Pottery:
The Sea of Names & the Pierced Inheritance

Anne Hamilton

Thank You

Dell
Rose
Donna
Quang
Ray
Milly
Wendy
Rhonda
Natalie
Kay

Remarkably relevant. The bar has been raised again with *God's Pottery*. My jaw had dropped and mind was blown after just a few pages in! If you are familiar with Anne Hamilton's previous books, or, if this is your first time, what an introduction.

God's Pottery will take you by the hand and lead you through new levels of insight and fresh inspiration at the intricacies of God. Her approachable writing style is a true joy to read, yet her words carry a reverence and the weight of truth that mirrors Jesus teaching style. The timely richness of revelation in this book is priceless.

A little word of advice, get 2 copies! Because if you are anything like me, mine is now filled with underlinings and scribbled notes. It is so good that, you want to be able to share it with friends but without letting go of your own precious copy.

Milly Bennitt
Cabin Academy

To *assume* is to 'take for granted'. To assume about God, the Creator of the Heavens and earth, is to take Him for granted.

To presume about God is even worse, for us that is, because we are far more likely to act on our presumptions. When I act on my presumptions about God, it means that I take upon myself something or someone without His permission or His authority—there is overstepping of His bounds.

The prophet Isaiah described this blindness aptly: *'O your contrariness! Will the potter be esteemed as clay? Will the work say of Him who made it, He did not make me? Or will the thing framed say of Him who framed it, He had no understanding?'* (Isaiah 29:16) And again: *'But now, Lord,*

You are our Father. We are the clay and You are our potter, and we all are the work of Your hand.' (Isaiah 64:8)

Recognise this and you are positioned to enter and partake His banquet of rare revelation presented in *God's Pottery*.

I have, and I've come away full. Shalom be with you,

Kwong Hii
Chairperson, *Vision 101*

Names are not just labels or codes. When I ask people, 'What does your name mean?' many answer that their names do not have any meaning. I wonder why. When I look at most names, I can see how they represent the hopes and dreams of parents for their children to be prosperous, and also to call out their destiny.

Lots of people change their names. In my culture, some even buy new names so that they may have a 'better' life and a 'new destiny'. But in the end, they find this is empty hope, a dry wishing well.

Don't think that your name is bad or negative. No! Through our names, God gives us His breath, His love, His psalm, His poetry and His blessing. Once we find out God's perspective about our names, we see Hi most beautiful and purposeful design.

'For I AM knows the thoughts, plans and intentions that I AM thinking toward you, says the Lord, thoughts of peace and not of evil, to give you a future and hope.' (Jeremiah 29:11)

Can the clay tell the Potter, 'Don't make me like the others because I don't want us all to look the same'? Externally, clay does look and feel the same—but, in the Master's hands, each is unique. Each of us is so individual that we have one-off fingerprints. The same Master created snowflakes so that not one snowflake is like another. Draw closer to God and He draws closer to you. God will reveal what His thoughts, plans and intentions are when He created you. Why don't you embark on this journey with Him?

I am truly blessed because I have set out on this journey through from *God's Poetry* all the way to *God's Pottery*.

Donna Ho
Director, *The Association of China, Israel and Australia Friendship, Culture and Economic Exchange*

I am as gob-smacked by the revelation and scholarship contained in *God's Pottery* as I have been in previous books in the series. I will be re-reading it in order to work on myself (with the help of the Holy Spirit). But first I must read *God's Pageantry*! After reading God's Poetry, I recognised that threshold guardians had a real hold in my life but I had no idea what that really meant. I am so grateful to be tackling that with the aid of *God's Pageantry* & *God's Pottery*! Thank you, Anne, for your obedience to Holy Spirit and diligence to serve the Body of Christ through these books.

Rhonda Pooley
Author, *Cambodian Harvest*

On reading *God's Pottery*, I became acutely aware how many people owe their allegiance to Mithras the god of the contract and not to Yahweh, Lord of the covenant. Instead of moving into our calling we labour painfully at jobs. Anne shows us how to move into that calling by getting rid of toxic shame and pride.

In this new work, she explains the meaning of the name and threshold covenants as outlined in the Bible at the Transfiguration of Jesus and elsewhere. She details the ways we reap consequences of actions in our family line and shows us how to be free of half kept promises, unfulfilled hopes, false forgiveness and hidden motives.

This is a transforming book on how to respond to the covenant Christ holds out for us.

Wendy Sargeant
Editor and Author, *Tyrannosaurus Wrecks*

My prayer is that what Anne has revealed in *God's Pottery* would continue to take the readers on a journey closer to the heart of Abba Father. I hope that, just as I have experienced, you may also be drawn into new depths of revelation and intimacy with the Father. Anne's books are a wonderful compilation that inspire a sense of mystery, awe, and fascination that has been lost through much of our modern understanding of biblical theology; she helps create new mindsets and freedom from this age of fear and anxiety. I dream of reading these books in a cabin in the mountains with a bowl of hot pumpkin soup and no interruptions! I want to pack these insights into my memory so they don't become distant in the busyness of daily life. I am so glad Anne keeps writing because I keep wanting to read these books over and over again.

Natalie Tensen
Co-Founder, *LeaderHeart.org*

Scripture quotations marked HNV are taken from the Hebrew Names Version of the Bible. Public domain.

Scripture quotations marked KJV are taken from the King James Version of the Bible. Public domain.

Scripture quotations marked NASB are taken from the New American Standard Bible®, Copyright © 1960, 1962, 1963, 1968, 1971, 1972, 1973, 1975, 1977, 1995 by The Lockman Foundation. Used by permission. (www.Lockman.org)

Scripture quotations marked NLT are taken from the Holy Bible, New Living Translation, copyright 1996, 2004. Used by permission of Tyndale House Publishers, Inc., Wheaton, Illinois 60189. All rights reserved.

Scripture quotations marked NIV are taken from the HOLY BIBLE, NEW INTERNATIONAL VERSION®. Copyright © 1973, 1978, 1984 Biblica. Used by permission of Zondervan. All rights reserved.

Scripture quotations marked NKJV are taken from the New King James Version. Copyright © 1982 by Thomas Nelson, Inc. Used by permission. All rights reserved.

Scripture quotations marked NRS are taken from New Revised Standard Version of the Bible, copyright 1952 [2nd edition, 1971] by the Division of Christian Education of the National Council of the Churches of Christ in the United States of America. Used by permission. All rights reserved.

Scripture quotations marked TPT are taken from The Passion Translation™, copyright © 2011. Used by permission of 5 Fold Media, LLC, Syracuse NY 13039, United States of America. All rights reserved.

IN THIS SERIES

God's Poetry: *The Identity & Destiny Encoded in Your Name*

God's Panoply: *The Armour of God & the Kiss of Heaven*

God's Pageantry: *The Threshold Guardians & the Covenant Defender*

By the same author

Many-Coloured Realm

The Singing Silence

The Winging Word

The Listening Land

Gawain and the Four Daughters of God:
the testimony of mathematics in Cotton Nero A.x

Daystar: The Days are Numbered Book 1

Contents

Foreword		xv
Prologue		xvii
1	From Name to Shame	1
2	We are all Eve	15
3	Seams of Gold	35
4	Trading in Names	61
5	The Sea of Names	75
6	Sentinels on the Threshold	95
7	Fourteen Steps	135
Appendices		153
Endnotes		165

Foreword

IN THE LATE NINETEENTH CENTURY, Henry Clay Trumball mentioned several times in his books that he intended to write a volume on name covenants. As far as I'm aware, it was never completed. His most famous works detail the blood, salt and threshold covenants as they were practised up to his own time. While he sometimes drew theological conclusions, the books are mainly anthropological and cultural in emphasis.

It would be wrong to suggest this book is the missing volume on name covenants. For a start, my emphasis is different: it's devotional and spiritual. However, because name covenants and the threshold covenants associated with them are such unfamiliar territory for most people, it inevitably brings theology into play.

This book, while introducing considerable new material, is effectively a summation of the series so far. It looks again at the nature of names as described in *God's Poetry*. It touches briefly on the armour of God as featured in *God's Panoply*. Mostly however, it builds on *God's Pageantry*, further developing the concept of a threshold covenant. It explores the constriction and wasting associated with that covenant in greater detail and exposes the array of spirits responsible.

Like the other books in this series, it has a hidden mathematical structure. I love using the numerical patterns of Scripture as a template. Also like my other books, it does not follow a strictly logical sequence. I may not be able to throw off the mental chains of Greek rationalism in favour of Hebrew block-thinking, but I've given it my best shot through a kaleidoscopic shuffle.

However even that got thrown aside for Chapter 5, *The Sea of Names*. I took time out. To be honest, I doubted the wisdom of writing a whole book on the machinations of evil. So I deliberately spent a whole chapter spotlighting the majesty of God.

Otherwise, we might just forget that evil simply counterfeits and perverts His works. And we might further forget that the battle is His, not ours.

Anne Hamilton

Prologue

IN A HOSPITAL IN SINGAPORE, a small boy lay dying. His doctors had ordered dozens of tests but could not determine the cause of his illness. All they knew was that the boy was sinking rapidly. In desperation his parents called an elderly Chinese physician, hoping his wealth of experience might provide an answer where the young, western-trained specialists had failed.

The old man talked to the parents, listened to their story, asked questions about the medical history on both sides of the family. At last he turned to the anxious father and gave a startling diagnosis. 'The problem is the boy's name.'

The parents were perplexed.

'It is too weighty for him,' the old man explained. 'He cannot carry it and is being crushed by the burden.'

Still the parents did not understand.

'You are a taxi-driver,' the old man said to the father. 'And you a cook...' to the mother. 'All your parents—the boy's grandparents—are peasant farmers. But you have named him a king.'

A light-bulb went on in the father's mind. 'Ahhh! His name is too heavy for his destiny.'

The physician nodded.

Not long after, the boy—now with a new name—recovered fully.

For the western-trained specialists, the improvement in his health was as mysterious as his illness had been. For surely—*surely?*—a change of name could not make such a miraculous difference.

The beginning of wisdom is to call things by their right names.

Chinese proverb

1

From Name to Shame

LIFE BEGINS WITH A NAME. In a world dominated by scientific explanations, that statement seems discordant, if not completely false. However, before the end of this book, I hope to have demonstrated science and Scripture are in greater harmony than we might suspect. Life is powered by a name.

Back in the second chapter of Genesis, the creation of mankind is described:

*And the Lord God formed man of the dust of the ground, and breathed into his nostrils the breath [*nashamah*] of life; and man became a living soul.*

Genesis 2:7 HNV

In this passage, *breath* translates 'nashamah' and it creates *soul*—'nephesh' here, but in other places 'neshama'. The intimate relationship between *breath* and *soul* is therefore clear to Jewish teachers but rarely to readers of other cultures.

Christians tend to look towards an entirely different Hebrew word relating *breath* to *spirit*: 'ruach'. First mentioned when the Spirit of God broods over the face of the deep, 'ruach' means *spirit*, *wind* and *breath*. Less familiar is 'neshima' for *breathing*, or the related term, 'neshama', *soul*.

By focussing on 'ruach' rather than 'nashamah', we miss a subtle nuance. Hidden like a kernel within 'nashamah', 'neshima' and 'neshama', the rabbis noticed 'shem', the Hebrew word for *name*.[1]

Influenced by scientific rationalism, we might regard this as simply random chance. But in Hebrew every letter has sacred significance: the words for *breathing* and *soul* contain *name*, 'shem', because a soul is conceived by naming.

God imparts life and soul by breathing a name over us. We are word made flesh.

'Adam,' He breathed, giving soul to the first human.[2]

God breathes life into our souls, so the rabbis reasoned, not simply through naming us but by giving us part of His own name.[3] I am inclined to think this surmise of the rabbis is correct. Why else would so many Eastern religions have breathing exercises which invoke the name of a god? Such a practice is an attempt to supplant the identity and destiny the Father whispered to our unformed frame, as He knitted each of us together in our mother's womb.

Parents have a chance to confirm this divine prophecy spoken over us. Their responsibility as caretakers of names comes from God himself.

It is an inheritance from Adam who was given dominion over naming. How important is this authority? Since it is the first of all gifts given to mankind, apart from life itself, we might suspect it is supreme in its significance. It precedes the gift of gender, the gift of a mate, the gift of work, the gift of choice, the gift of stewardship of the earth.

In naming the animals, Adam reflected the image of God, the One who named him.

We were made from dust
a bit of earth kissed by heaven
and we are made
to be ground breakers
and peacemakers
and freedom shakers.

Ann Voskamp

The responsibility of the caretakers of names is an enormous one. Every name speaks out both identity and destiny: it tells us who we are and what we are asked to mend in this broken world. It encodes calling and meaning.

As we grow, there is a transfer of authority. The power of our name comes into our own keeping.

My friend Janette has experienced enormous difficulty in trying to persuade people to pronounce her name correctly. Some people are irritated by what they see as her needless and pedantic insistence on getting it right. Why should she care? But for her, it's a matter of identity. There's an enormous difference between Janette and Jenette: the first is called to be a gate-keeper, the second a wave-rider.

The ancient world understood names to be charged with almost unimaginable power. A knowledge of names was an almost magical endowment for a scholar: to know the name of a god enabled him to summon and control that god.

Finnish folklore contains the idea of the 'word of origin': to control or banish an evil spirit, it was necessary to know and announce its proper name, as well as relate to it the history of its creation.

The names of spirits—and deities in particular—were therefore kept secret. In some tribes, it was treason to speak them. If an enemy discovered the names of the clan gods, then those protecting divinities could be lured away and the people conquered. The Romans were notorious for seeking out the names of the gods in territories they coveted. Using an incantation called *elicio*—from which we get the word 'elicit'—they would offer various tribal gods inducements to come to a splendid new temple by the river Tiber.

Did the Romans ever find out the name of the God of the Hebrews? Perhaps; but I'm inclined to doubt it. Even today, the name is well-hidden behind the common epithet, Yahweh. That name both reveals and conceals the actual word God gave to Moses. Yahweh actually means *He is who He is*, not *I am who I am*.

I was startled the first time I delved into the Hebrew of Exodus 3:14. I thought there was a serious typographical error. 'Ehyeh' isn't the same as 'Yahweh'.

Nor is it the name God gave to Abraham. The first recorded name by which God revealed Himself to mankind shows His maternal character. El Shaddai means *the strong-breasted one*, the sustainer and nurturer.

My favourite 'selfie' from God is, however, not the *strong-breasted one*. It's Yahweh Nissi, *the Lord my Banner*, and running it a close second is the *one with the long nose*.

Isn't that so wonderfully unpretentious? Majesty with the long nose! You'll find this strange expression mentioned when God passed in front of Moses and showed him His back. There, not long after the incident with the golden calf, He proclaimed: *'The Lord, the Lord, the compassionate and gracious God, slow to anger, abounding in love...'* (Exodus 34:6 NIV)

That phrase translated *slow to anger*—or in other versions *long-suffering*—is more literally rendered the *long-nosed one* or the *one of long breathing*.

The metaphor of the long nose and slow breathing reminds us that, to image our Maker, we should not make haste when it comes to anger. There's godly wisdom in the admonition to stop when we're angry, count to ten and take long, slow breaths.

The Lord as banner, uplifter and exalter is also embedded in 'nashamah', *breath*.

Breath is therefore about *life*, *uplift*, *name* and *soul*.

Name is so important in Scripture that it was one of the four covenants that Abraham undertook. These in order were blood, name, threshold and salt.

Name was also one of the four covenants Jesus enacted during the night before His death.

It's not a label, nor a convenient means of identifying people and differentiating one from another: it's power.

And the enemy of our souls wants that power. He wants to divert us from the identity and destiny God has prophetically breathed into our lives. And which our parents, generally speaking, have confirmed. For, despite the true story of the boy from Singapore, I personally believe most parents get it mostly right.[4]

God is the breath inside the breath.

Kabīr

The Chinese word for *family name* is 'shen'.

Linguistically it's hardly a nudge away from the Hebrew word for *name*, 'shem'. In time, Yahweh—the euphemism for the name of God, Ehyeh—became as sacred as the name itself. So, to avoid this new hallowed name and ensure they would not even accidentally pronounce its sacred syllables, the Jewish people began to call God 'HaShem', *The Name*.

The breathy 'h' Abram and Sarai received when they exchanged names with God was considered to be an abbreviation of HaShem. Let's pause for a moment and consider the mind-warping implications of what happened when they became Abraham and Sarah. They actually exchanged names with God who, on this very occasion, revealed Himself for the first time as El Shaddai.

Now, personally I think the 'h' in both Abraham and Sarah's names comes from Ehyeh, not HaShem. However its origin is not particularly important. What is important is the exchange of names: this means a name covenant has been sealed.

It also means that Abraham and Sarah were called into oneness with God through their names. Still, it seems strange. If God breathed life into Abram through naming, then hadn't He already given him a name a hundred years—an entire century—before he became Abraham?

Yes, He had. But in saying that most parents get it *mostly* right in confirming the prophecy of names, they often don't get it *exactly* right. Even if they do, that doesn't take away from us freedom of choice.

We are summoned into our destiny through our names but we are not fated to achieve it. We can turn away from it.

The oldest name for God in Chinese is 'ShangDi' which, thousands of years ago, seems to have been pronounced very close to the oldest Hebrew name for God: 'Shaddai'. In modern Chinese, 'shen' is not only the word for *family name* but also the word for *God* and for *spirit*.[5]

The Chinese share the Jewish understanding that names come from God and are sacred and life-giving. They also share an understanding of choice. Who has dominion of a surname? Who is its covenant with—the triune God who created names? Or a dark spirit who'd like nothing better than to siphon off their power and leave us without a destiny or inheritance?

Paul wrote to the Ephesians, the people most attuned to spiritual power in the ancient world:

...I fall on my knees before the Father, from whom every family in heaven and on earth receives its true name.

Ephesians 3:14–15 GNT

The power of names has been lost to people of the west, and increasingly to those of the east. Even if we believe that names are more than labels, our increasing secularisation pressures us into acting differently. The choices built within names go unnoticed, the fork in the road on the hero's journey drifts by unrecognised, a haze of frustration or depression obscures our high calling.

We miss the fact that naming is the power to create.

In Chinese, the ideogram for 'create' is composed of *dust, mouth, life* and *person* fully formed and *walking*. Its characters actually spell out the creation of mankind, just as we saw in Genesis.

*And the Lord God **formed man** of the **dust** of the ground, and **breathed** into his nostrils the breath of **life**; and man became a living soul.*

Genesis 2:7 HNV

The emphasis in Chinese might be slightly different from Hebrew but the essence is the same.

Our names are meant to be hidden, protected and nurtured within the name of God. In the modern world, they are no longer the power that summons us into our destiny. We have forfeited our inheritance to an enemy who has used it to enslave us.

When Paul says Scriptures are 'God-breathed' or 'inspired', he is suggesting they are 'in-Spirited'... they are life-giving. For where the Spirit is, there is life. God breathed upon the dust—that glorified mudball called Adam—and he became a living being. He came alive because God's breath was in him.

Dwight Pryor, *Jesus—The Fullness of Tanakh*

All over the world, creativity is stifled in mind-numbing jobs; very few people get to enjoy using the creative power their own name calls them to use. Christians are called to mend the broken world through their work.

The word 'labour' for *work* in English comes from the Old French for *pain*. In Hebrew, however, 'labour' comes from the word for *angel*. Work should be satisfying, uplifting, upbuilding, heavenly—otherwise we are denying our own name.

Work and worship should be hand in hand, fingers entwined, moving in an easy, dancing rhythm together.

Too many of us tend to think of worship as simply songs—sometimes even a specific kind of song—when it is really about offering a sacrifice of praise to God. The Hebrew people considered the study of the Torah to be the highest form of worship.

To conduct a worship audit of our lives, we simply need to ask ourselves where we are investing the most time. Particularly the most voluntary time. Where are we investing the most money? Particularly when it comes to free capital.

Have we polluted God's holy altar—or worse, still—even created an alternative altar with teraphim, *household gods*, of our own making? And kept covenant with them, rather than with the One who breathed life and destiny into us by whispering our names?

Covenant is one of the most misunderstood concepts in Christianity today. No, actually, I retract that. It is *the* most misunderstood concept of our time.

Writers who are otherwise scrupulous in explaining the meaning behind Scriptural symbols talk loosely about the 'covenant of the tithe' or the 'sandal covenant'—to name just two.

In doing so, they totally confuse the ideas of contract and covenant, using language that makes them seem almost indistinguishable. Many people today view a covenant as no different from an exclusive contract: an agreement, an accord, a pledge, a pact that you can only get out of by recourse to serious legal representation.

Sure, a covenant has many legal overtones: exchanges and vows, oaths and obligations. But it is as far above a contract as the stars are beyond the treetops.

A contract to buy a car does not bind your identity to the seller's. To even imagine that is a fairly horrifying thought! Such a contract does not give you the dignity or the destiny of the seller, nor will you find yourself instantly adopted into the seller's family. Nor does it mean that, should the seller be robbed of what you paid, you have a responsibility to come to his aid.

All of which apply to covenant.

The essential nature of covenant is oneness. In becoming one with another person, such as in a blood brotherhood ceremony, a transcendent quality comes into play. This soars beyond fulfilment of duty, debt or a desire to be dependable. It's about wholeness rather than aloneness. It's about surrender of self rather than the sacrifice of the communal which, in our era, has been so perversely admired as rugged individualism. Perversely, because it is covenant that asks of us a risk as high as heaven itself.

Marriage was designed as a covenant, not a contract. Although there are many vows, what differentiates it from a simple legal agreement is two persons becoming one.

This is why it gives a wrong impression to talk of the 'covenant of the tithe' or the 'sandal covenant': tithes may be an obligation under a covenant and a sandal exchange may constitute a legal bargain but neither of these is about two individuals becoming one.

Abraham undertook four covenants with God during his lifetime: blood was the first, probably on the slopes of Mount Hermon. Fourteen years later in Hebron the name covenant followed. Six days[6] after that, the threshold and salt covenants were enacted. None of these covenants had anything to do with the offering of Isaac at Mount Moriah because all of them occurred before he was born.

Jesus undertook the same four covenants with His disciples during the night before His death: blood, salt, name and threshold.

Of these, name and threshold covenants are virtually unknown in Christian circles today. Most believers have at least heard of the blood covenant and salt covenant, even if they mistakenly view them as an exclusive contract, rather than as oneness.

The consequence of this lack of knowledge is, as Hosea so succinctly prophesied, destruction. Too many people owe their allegiance to Mithras, god of the contract, and not to Yahweh, lord of the covenant.

Too many people have name covenants with unholy deities; so they labour painfully at a job instead of moving angelically in their calling.

A rich man knew he was dying, but he hated the thought of leaving his hard-earned wealth behind. He had all his assets converted to gold bars, put them in a huge bag on his bed and, when he sensed he was breathing his last, draped his body over the bag. At the gate of Heaven, St. Peter was very surprised see the bag. 'Wow! You managed to get up here with something from earth! This is a first! Let's see what you brought.' He opened the bag, then looked in perplexity at the man. 'You brought... street paving?!'

Another rich man died and approached the Pearly Gates. St. Peter told him heaven was getting unexpectedly crowded, so he had to test people, by using a point system. If the rich man got to 100 points he could enter.

The man told Peter he went to church every Sunday. Peter gave him one point. The man mentioned that he'd given regularly to the poor and had even helped start a soup kitchen in his town. Peter marked him down for another point.

The man thought again, then said he gave tithes to his church. Peter added a point. The man, desperately searching his memory, finally said he'd only sworn twice in his life. Peter added half a point. Never stolen anything. One point. Never killed anyone. Another point. Been married for fifty years to the same woman and never cheated on her or looked with lust on another woman. Three points.

'Three points!' the rich man gasped. He realised he hadn't even cracked double figures in the points tally. 'At this rate,' he said in frustration, 'I'll only get in by the grace of God.'

Peter smiled and flung the gate open wide. 'Come on in!'

Many jokes exist about St Peter guarding the gates of heaven and these are two I particularly like. The last one is even theologically sound. Of all the saints who could have become associated with door-keeping, it's ironically been assigned to the one with 'door problems' throughout Scripture. Yet Peter is the archetypal threshold name.

Jewish tradition tells a different story of the gates of heaven. There an angel stands guard. His task is to ask a simple question. If the soul wanting admittance to heaven can give the right answer, the gates will swing wide. But if not, the soul will be turned away.

Here's the question: *'Who are you?'*

It's not a trick question. All we have to do is to remember the name God breathed into us when He gave us a soul. That whisper of love is more than simply naming: it is a divine prophecy of both our identity and our destiny.

If we have obeyed the summons of that prophecy, we will have worked at our true calling during our lifetime. But if we have turned aside from our destiny, then we will have forgotten who we really are. We won't recall our true name when the angel asks for it.

Forgetting is not simply failing to remember. Once we realise that remember means *put back together again*, it's easy to recognise its opposite: *dismember*.

Forgetting is dismembering who we are; it's a mutilation of our identity and destiny.

Trauma and terror can cause us to forget. But a far more common reason for dismembering of memories is guilt. Guilt makes us want to forget. So does shame.

Although guilt is not precisely the same as shame, they are closely related. One leads to the other. In fact, the English word *ashamed* comes from the Hebrew word for *guilt*, "asham".[7]

Guilt is the cause of shame; though I want to be careful to qualify this statement. The reverse is not true. Shame is the result of guilt but not necessarily our own guilt—some people are so crafty and manipulative that they can project shame onto an innocent party and make it stick. Shame can result from someone else's guilt.

Shame can also cause us to take dismembered memories and re-arrange them to protect our self-image. In an active partnership with the spirit of forgetting, some people rewrite their own personal history and come to believe the new version. They could pass a lie detector test.

The spirit of forgetting is Hell's perennial Employee of the Month. A person who is tempted may fall, but he may also resist or repent. But people who have dismembered their memories can't repent because they've forgotten their sin.

In forgetting what they've actually done—or neglected to do—they create a false view of their own character and forget who they really are. Not only that, they forget who God calls them to be.

Their identity and destiny are thrown aside by an imperative need to assuage any feelings of guilt, turn the situation around mentally and protect their self-image as righteous, blameless and innocent.

This process can be teased out through "asham', *guilt*.

Like 'nashamah', *breath*, and 'neshama', *soul*, it contains 'shem', *name*. The Hebrew prefix 'a means *I will*.

So, if we consider 'shem' as a verb, the word, "asham', for *guilt* could be translated *I will name*.[8]

Is this what guilt amounts to? Rebellious self-determination that by saying, 'I will name,' really means: *I will choose my own destiny, I will decide who I am and what I am meant to be, I will see myself in whatever way I wish, I will do it my way, I will not have anyone else impose their choices on me, I will live free of prophecy, I will be the master of my fate, the captain of my soul.*

Perhaps even a step beyond that last thought: *I will create my own soul.*

If it seems harsh or even callous to describe those locked in shame as prideful and rebellious, it's important to realise that shame involves a rejection of God's forgiveness. A feeling of deep unworthiness accompanies shame but this is not the same as humility.

A humble attitude acknowledges sinfulness but allows us to receive the grace of God, despite our guilt. However shame-riddled unworthiness causes us to shun the grace of God and frustrate His purposes for us.

...do not frustrate the grace of God: for if righteousness comes by the law, then Christ is dead in vain.

Galatians 2:21 KJV

A sense of unworthiness easily becomes entwined with identity. We name ourselves anew:

'I am worthless.'
'I am hopeless.'
'I am a loser.'
'I am no good.'
'I am a deadbeat.'
'I am unloveable.'
'I am a mistake.'

These statements may not look like enthronements of self. Certainly they're not in the league of those people whose core belief is:

'I am perfect.'
'I am faultless.'
'I am the best.'
'I am fantastic.'
'I am god-like.'

It's much more subtle than that. It is holding to a belief that settles into defiance of the love of God—who loved us enough to die for us. In believing that we are worthless and in refusing to affirm we are fearfully and wonderfully created as His masterpiece, His poetry and His symphony, we come into agreement with the lies of the Enemy. We make an alliance with the Evil One. Whenever he accuses us before the throne of God, we accept his lies about us instead of accepting God's forgiveness.

In holding on to shame, however furtively or secretly, we abide in sin and fail to fulfil our purpose and calling.

Sure we can see sin as missing the mark. Or as falling short of perfection. Or even as, according to the English etymology pointed out in *God's Panoply*, perpetuating a cycle of revenge and unforgiveness.

But how does sin—falling short of the divine standard—affect our names, those carriers of identity and destiny? It's simple.

Sin is treason against our own names.

2

We are all Eve

SIN IS A BETRAYAL too of God's name, but we're apt to lose the impact of its ruinous nature when we express ourselves in a more commonplace theology. 'Missing the mark' doesn't always convey the calamitous nature of sin in our hearts.

However, if we look at the words related to *guilt*, we have a better idea of the consequences of sin: *ruin* in Hebrew, 'yasham', is a result of "asham", *guilt*. Another result is 'meshammah', *horror, destruction, waste.*

But then how do we reconcile sin as being a betrayal of God's name with the extraordinary, plenipotentiary authority God gave Adam to name the animals? The fact is, the power and privilege of naming was given to mankind prior to the first rebellion. It is now part of a tainted creation; names are therefore corrupted and as much in need of restoration as any creature.

And perhaps it is because of the damage done to name that God instituted name covenants—such as the name exchange that occurred when God's name, El Shaddai, was revealed for the first time and Abram became Abraham. Another such name exchange occurred when Jesus' title, Messiah, was spoken with definitive faith for the first time. Simon offered Jesus the name 'Messiah' and Jesus offered him back Cephas/Peter.

Name covenants carry such huge potential for blessing it is no wonder the Enemy has claimed them in an attempt to pervert their benefits and turn them into a curse.

The commandment given at Sinai—*you shall not take the name of the Lord your God in vain*—really says we should not lift up the name of

God as if it were trivial, as if it means nothing. We should not disgrace it, nor betray it.

Yet, the truth is, every sin betrays it.

Hence the extraordinary grace of covenant. God exchanges names, taking on to Himself the bleakness, the ruin and the desolate shambles of the names given to us and offering us a resurrected identity and destiny.

Guilt... is feeling bad about one's actions, but shame is feeling bad about oneself.

Gregory Boyle, *Tattoos on the Heart: The Power of Boundless Compassion*

If there's one thing worse than a job which stifles creativity, it's no job at all. And no hope of one. Ever.

Gregory Boyle writes about the gangs of Los Angeles, revealing that their members don't plan their futures, they plan their funerals. With nothing to live for—with no prospect of change—life has no purpose.

The intrinsic spiritual relationship between not only shame and name but also addiction and name is revealed in his book, *Tattoos on the Heart*. Shame, he says, quoting John Bradshaw, is at the root of all addictions, including the gang addiction. Guilt, he goes on, is feeling bad about our actions, but shame is feeling bad about ourselves.

Henry Malone asserts that guilt says, 'I *made* a mistake,' but shame says, 'I *am* a mistake.'

Follow the line here: addiction is caused by shame and shame is a sense of badness or misshapenness about ourselves. A sense of complete badness about ourselves means we've been starved of love and cannot give what we've never had: we can't love our neighbours or ourselves.[9]

Follow this line a little while longer: to be loved is to be known. Known, appreciated and celebrated for who we are.

'Who doesn't want to be called by name, known?' Boyle asks as he reveals story after story of kids whose transformation began with an electric moment when they were recognised by name. *'The "knowing" and the "naming" seem to get at what Anne Lamott calls our "inner sense of disfigurement". As misshapen as we feel ourselves to be, attention from another reminds of our true shape in God... Names are important. After all, the main occupation of most gang members most of the time is the writing of their <u>names</u> on walls.'*

When we look at graffiti disfiguring around our cities, it's often hard to see that, in each spraypainted tag, each wild signature, each wall-blazoned name, is a cry to be loved and known.

Gangs are imitations of true community. Poor simulations of covenant and oneness.

But let's face it: most churches are poor simulations of covenant and oneness too. It's easy to be down on gangs but churches haven't exactly been role models.

Each person is called to be the City of God, corporate with Him. Instead we tend to hang on grimly by our fingernails and refuse to surrender our rights to separateness. We make a rugged fortress of our individuality, fence our heart and reject any connection to the Body.

As gangs (or churches) can be the very opposite of community, so 'naming and shaming' is the very opposite of what naming was originally meant to be: an expression of love.

Name covenants even more so. The name exchange in such a covenant says: 'I love you so much that I give you my identity, my destiny, my future.'

In a name covenant with God, shame is lifted, guilt removed, love is a leaping delight, addiction vanishes—all because He has our names in His keeping.

But, for many Christians, I may as well be describing a fairytale. Shame and its child, addiction, are a daily reality and have been for so long that, like the gang members in LA, there's nothing to hope for. Nothing's ever going to change.

If you've said that, or even thought it, perhaps it's time to consider a different question: How can a name covenant go so madly, badly and dangerously wrong?

And when someone else speaks your name you feel pleased. You feel wanted. You feel there. Alive. Even if they're saying your name with dislike, at least you know you're you, that you exist.

Aidan Chambers, *Nik: Now I Know*

Shame is not all bad, though there's a tendency to think it is. Our modern secular society has worked very hard to remove shame from sexuality and any variation in its expression, from having an abortion, from nudity in public, from cheating in marriage, even from dishonesty and theft. Instead it's now all about 'getting caught out' in some situations or 'saying the wrong thing' in others.

When we take shame away, then sin should disappear—so our new social thinking goes. It's like trying to remove the symptoms and believing the underlying disease will simply vanish. A conscience can become seared through repeatedly ignoring it—or we can basically turn it off. We want to have fun and, even if the only voice cautioning us is the one inside, we choose to flick the switch and silence it.

The purpose of shame is to alert us to our own guilt. A sense of shame reveals an innate wrongness in a situation, even if no one has told us so.

When guilt or discipline makes no impact, sometimes shame does.

Back in the days when I was the coordinator of Year 8 Mathematics at a large provincial high school, I often had difficult students. One of the most disruptive was a girl who would giggle loudly, sing at the top of her voice, flirt with the boys nearby and call out to those on the far side of the room trying desperately to avoid her. She'd also shoot paper planes across the desks and generally disrupt every lesson. Some days would start out calm before a sudden eruption, and some days were just wall-to-wall mayhem. She was supposed to have ADHD—but personally I thought she just wanted to have fun.

On parent-teacher night, I explained the situation to her mother who sighed and said she'd had the same story from all the other teachers. I detailed the disciplinary tactics I'd attempted—without the slightest success. Her mum confided that she herself suspected the doctor's diagnosis might not be accurate. Then I told her mother I'd come up with a plan to find out whether her daughter had ADHD or not. I enlisted her help to put it into action—though, as I told her, I suspected it might never come to the point of needing her to carry out what I proposed.

The next day, I spoke to the girl before class. 'Your mum and I are very worried about you. You're failing maths at the moment and, if things go on like they have, you may never be able to catch up on all the work you've missed. You're such a bright student it would be a pity to see you go into the lowest class next year.'

The girl gave me her usual mocking smirk.

'So, because we're both so concerned,' I went on, 'and your mum wants to do her best for you, she's going to be coming into class once a week just to sit next to you and help you. She'd like to be able to come in every day but she won't be able to get the time off work. But she'll be able to get Wednesday afternoons off so that's when she's coming in, starting tomorrow.'

The smirk had long since disappeared into a white-faced look of utter horror.

'What do I have to do,' the girl gasped, 'so that this won't happen?'

I sent her off to her seat with two words: 'Be perfect.'

At the end of the lesson, I kept her back after the rest of the class had gone. 'I have good news,' I told her, 'and bad news.'

She looked wary.

'The good news is that I'll phone your mum and tell her that she doesn't need to come in tomorrow. The bad news is that now I know you can be perfect. Now I know you can control your own actions and I'm going to hold you responsible for your behaviour. So, if you aren't perfect from now on, I'll be on the phone to your mum straight away. And guess what's going to happen?'

The threat was enough. For the next two weeks, the girl was indeed perfect in every maths class. And after that time, she was normal. Neither incredibly disruptive nor impeccably good.

The prospect of shame in front of her peers was enough to break her destructive cycle of behaviour. Guilt made no difference. Neither did discipline. Or parental concern.

But shame did.

Most of the time, shame is a poison. But, like arsenic in small doses, it can be beneficial. It's toxic when it gets out of hand.

Shame, says Henry Malone, is an *identity thief*. In fact, that's the title of his brilliant book.

He discusses two kinds of shame: true shame and false shame.

The first is a consequence of guilt and is meant to drive us into our heavenly Father's arms, bawling for forgiveness. But often we're overtaken by false shame—a lethal feeling that drives us away from God. We may believe that, because shame and humiliation are so closely allied, that humility is the issue. But in fact the root cause of toxic shame is pride: the sin of the guardian cherub we call Lucifer.

Ken Bailey worked in the Middle East for some forty years. As often as he could, he asked the local people about the parables of Jesus. He wanted to know what unspoken cultural nuances there were in the stories that Western readers invariably missed. In particular, he was interested in how

Middle Eastern people viewed the parable of *'The Prodigal Son'*.

For a start, he discovered it had a different title: *'The Running Father'*. In Middle Eastern culture, running was considered humiliating for a middle-aged man—and lifting his robe to run, doubly so! This was such a startling aspect of the story it was worth mentioning in the title.

The father puts himself to shame to prevent shame being heaped on his son. In that culture, the locals would have understood what his return in rags meant: he'd lost everything. On entering his village, he would face the kezazah, *the cutting off*.[10] It was a ceremony of exile, reserved for those who lost their money amongst foreigners. A clay pot filled with burnt beans would be broken at his feet as a sign the community banished him forever.

In this story the father is willing to sacrifice his own honour. That's what our God is like; what He calls us to be like.

We are His poetry, but we are also His pottery.

Though He reserves the right to remould us on His wheel, He does not want us broken in pieces, destroyed by shame.

In Ephesians 2:10 NKJV, we're told: *For we are His workmanship, created in Christ Jesus for good works, which God prepared beforehand that we should walk in them.*

The Greek word which is translated *workmanship* comes from 'poeo', *poem*.

We are God's poems. When God breathes our names to give us a soul, He activates a poem. He embodies a spoken word as matter, making us flesh, just as once the Word became flesh.

As an activated word, with a prophesied identity and destiny enfolded in our name, we are more than simply spirit: in the conjoining of body, soul and spirit, God's poem becomes God's pottery:

Yet, O Lord, You are our Father. We are the clay, You are the potter; we are all the work of Your hand.

Isaiah 68:4 NIV

Regardless of our chips and flaws, our cracks and missing

shards, the unevenness of our finish or the crazing in our glaze, He regards us with delight:

...the holy ones in the land, they are the noble, in whom is all My delight.

Psalm 16:3 NRS

Even if we have been broken—mentally, emotionally, physically, spiritually—He wants to pick up each and every potsherd, even down to the tiniest chip, and restore us to our right design. Whatever the kezazah of man's devising, He knows how to fix it.

He Himself endured a kezazah, *a cutting off*, when Jesus was cut off from His friends, His family, His people at the time of His death:

...He was... cut off from the land of the living for the crimes of my people, who deserved the punishment themselves.

Isaiah 53:8 CJB

He endured the shame, took the punishment for the guilt—the 'asham—so His covenant friends don't have to. So that the Master Potter can take each fragment and rebuild the whole.

In 1974 farmers digging a well in Shaanxi Province, China, unearthed the remains of the now-famous terracotta warriors. The silent ranks on display at Mount Li today are earthenware depictions of generals, officers, foot-soldiers—all with individual features—dating back to the time of the first Emperor, Qin Shi Huang, about 2200 years ago. Perhaps most amazing of all is not the sight of this vast and awe-inspiring pottery army. Rather it is the knowledge each figure has been painstakingly rebuilt from crushed fragments—all that remained after a fire apparently caused the roof to collapse around two millennia ago.[11]

If such fine reconstruction is possible for expert conservators, imagine what God, the Master Potter, can do as you breathe in His holy name.

...out of the deepest sleep you can imagine, with the feeling that the voice she liked best in the world had been calling her name.

CS Lewis, *Prince Caspian: The Return to Narnia*

Then Joshua son of Nun secretly sent two spies from Shittim. 'Go, look over the land,' he said, 'especially Jericho.' So they went and entered the house of a prostitute named Rahab and stayed there.

Joshua 2:1 NIV

Thirty-eight years before Joshua sent these two scouts into Jericho, he had been a member of a party of twelve spies. This group had been sent by Moses to check out the land promised by God as an inheritance to the people of Israel. The majority of those twelve spies had brought back a negative report that had totally disheartened the people. Decades of desert wandering went by and virtually an entire generation had to pass away before God gave permission for a second attempt.

The two scouts who went to Jericho were men of a different kind. Although the Bible does not record how they managed to enter the Canaanite fortress, Jewish tradition says they disguised themselves as potters. 'Here are pots! Here are pots!' they cried. Among other things, say the rabbinic sages, these words reveal their essential attitude about themselves. They saw themselves primarily as pots for the will of God.

'An earthenware pot's only value is the ability to hold something,' says Yechiel Eckstein in commenting on this tradition. 'These men placed no value on their own egos. Rather, they saw their only value as serving as vessels for the will of God. The result was that they succeeded where others had failed.'[12]

We are truly like clay: the human body is composed of the same basic elements. Paul says that we hold this treasure in earthen vessels, (2 Corinthians 4:7 NKJV) but he also says that some vessels are for honour and some for dishonour (2 Timothy 2:20 NKJV). It is only as we participate with God in cleansing ourselves from dishonour that we become fit for the Master Potter's use.

More than that, as we allow God to remove shame and guilt from our lives, we not only become suitable vessels to carry His glory but we enable His will to be accomplished. Our value is not in our clay-like selves; it's not in the pottery of our person but in the Holy Spirit who fills each vessel to enable us to take possession of an imperishable inheritance.

When God, the Master Potter, draws us into name covenant, He not only takes our shame on Himself and exchanges it for the righteousness of Christ, He also prepares an inheritance for us. Hebrews 11:16 NIV is an amazing testimony to this: '...*Therefore God is not ashamed to be called their God, for He has prepared a city for them.*'

Alistair Petrie comments: 'This means He will endorse us, ratify us, protect us and even proclaim us in the heavenlies. God is not ashamed to be called our God. He is, in effect, surnaming Himself after us. Isaiah 45:4 RSV states: "*For the sake of My servant Jacob, and Israel My chosen, I call you by your name, I surname you though you do not know Me.*"

Take a moment to consider the implications. A name exchange is not just God taking our names as His own and giving us His. It is also taking our shame and humiliation, as well as our guilt and rebellion, our self-determination and inner disfigurement and offering us instead:

- nurture through the name, El Shaddai, *almighty* (Genesis 17:1)
- provision through the name, Jehovah Jireh, *the one who sees* (Genesis 22:14)
- eternal life through the name, Ehyeh, I am who I am, *the everliving one* (Exodus 3:14)
- exclusivity and passionate love through the name, Qannan, *jealous* (Exodus 34:14)
- uplift, forgiveness and protection through the name, Jehovah Nissi, *banner* (Exodus 17:15)

When death cuts all other links, there remains the name. Baptism: the union of a soul with a name, the name it will carry into eternity.

JM Coetzee, *The Master of Petersburg*

Back in the beginning, before the first sin, God breathed life into the first man by whispering his name: Adam.

And the Lord God formed man [adam] of the dust of the ground [adamah], and breathed into his nostrils the breath [nashamah] of life; and man became a living soul [nephesh | neshama].

Genesis 2:7 HNV

His name reflects his origin and his destiny: to guard and protect the earth from which he emerged, to steward, care for and have dominion over it.

When it came time to create a mate for Adam, the Master Potter tried another method entirely. He put Adam into a deep sleep and took woman out of his side.

This was prophecy in action, its symbolism veiled for millennia.

Part of its sense could however have been grasped immediately by Adam. Woman, at that stage unnamed, was flesh of his flesh, bone of his bone and therefore also 'Adam'. By forming woman from one of Adam's ribs—the only bone that can easily regenerate—God ensured that Adam could never properly think of her as a separate being. They didn't even have different names: Adam didn't call his wife 'Eve' until after they'd been expelled from Eden.

Fortunately, the opportunity to become one again was never permanently lost. God made provision for it—through covenant.

Generally we tend to think of covenantal oneness as related to marriage—or sexual union. However, oneness is not only about flesh and is therefore not the sole preserve of those who are physically intimate. Any covenantal relationship including, for instance, that of an armour-bearer or blood brother, is in essence oneness.

There's further monumental significance in the birth of Eve.

In one sense, it's unique: no one else has ever been physically born this way.

Yet, in another sense, it isn't unique: God's action foreshadows the spiritual 'new birth' through Jesus.

This idea of 'new birth' stumped Nicodemus. He'd met secretly with Jesus and, instead of getting his questions answered, he received some cryptic statements about being reborn. The whole idea messed with his mind. Images of having to crawl back into his mother's womb surfaced.

So Jesus said: '*I tell you the truth, no one can enter the Kingdom of God unless he is born of water and the Spirit.*' (John 3:5 NIV)

No doubt Nicodemus was still baffled about this new allusion: what would the breaking of the waters of a spiritual childbirth look like? Would the Spirit's breath rename the child as blood issued forth?

CS Lewis is often quoted as saying, 'God is so masculine, that He makes all of creation seem feminine in comparison.' More accurately, he wrote: 'The masculine none of us can escape. What is above and beyond all things is so masculine that we are all feminine in relation to it.'

For years I felt this notion was as inscrutable as Jesus' comment about the new birth. And somehow related to it.

Fortunately John's Gospel is symmetrically arranged.

It starts and ends with 496: as Richard Bauckham has noted, the *Hymn to the Logos* is a 496-syllable poem and the epilogue is 496 words.

It starts and ends with 17: the first sentence about the Logos is 17 words while its last section features the 17th triangular number, 153.

It starts and ends with the testimony of a man named John: the Baptist is mirrored by 'the disciple Jesus loved'.[13]

It starts and ends with a sheep metaphor: the Baptist speaking of 'the Lamb of God' mirrors Jesus urging Peter, 'Feed My sheep'.

It starts and ends with a gathering of disciples[14] which includes

Nathanael and Simon Peter. Nathanael is never mentioned otherwise. Positioned like book-ends, his doubts as the narrative opens balance Thomas' doubts at the end. Both of them then proclaim the Lordship of Jesus. They may even have related names: Nathanael is widely thought to be the disciple elsewhere named Bartholomew—*son of Ptolemy*—and Thomas, as I have pointed out in *God's Pageantry*, is a name almost certainly derived from Ptolemy.

Deeper into this ring-like structure (technically called *chiasmus*) are two stories about different women named Mary. Next from the front comes the clearing of the temple. From the back, it's the empty tomb episode.

Then, back and front, Nicodemus appears.

The mirror positioning of each story tells us they are meant to inform and be understood in the light of each other.[15] In the case of Nicodemus, it's appropriate to examine the context. His final appearance occurs after this statement:

'...one of the soldiers pierced His side with a spear, and immediately blood and water came out.'

John 19:34 NIV

Now the word for *blood* in this verse is 'haima'—and it also means *spirit*.

Admittedly it's not the same word as used back in John 3:5 for *spirit*. That was 'pneuma'.

However, I believe we should consider the testimony of the chiasmus in the structural design. Nicodemus witnessed a breaking forth of water and blood/spirit, as Jesus had explained accompanied the new birth.

However birth doesn't normally occur through a man's pierced side. Only one similar instance occurs in all of history: Eve.

The prophetic symbolism of her birth was thus fulfilled: as woman was taken from the side of the first Adam, so the Bride was taken from the second Adam—Jesus Christ.

The Sea of Names & the Pierced Inheritance

'The male you could have escaped, for it exists only on the biological level. But the masculine none of us can escape. What is above and beyond all things is so masculine that we are all feminine in relation to it. You had better agree with your adversary quickly.'
'You mean I shall have to become a Christian?' said Jane.
'It looks like it,' said the Director.

CS Lewis, That Hideous Strength

The ring-like structure of John's Gospel is designed to unveil the identity of the Bride, then reinforce the supernatural nature of her birth. All Christian believers form the Bride and are therefore like Eve before she was named: one with Christ and Feminine in relation to the Masculine.

We are all Eve.

Uncomfortable as that notion might be to many Christian men, it's incontrovertible. We—the Body of Christ—together form the new Eve, the Bride of the second Adam.

The structural chiasmus testifies to this. The story of Mary failing to recognise the risen Christ in the garden is meant to inform—and be informed by—another story of a different Mary. The parallel to the post-resurrection conversation of Mary Magdalene and Jesus is the dialogue during the wedding feast at Cana. There Jesus, at the request of His mother, changed water into wine so the bridal party would not be embarrassed by a shortage.

The language in the garden encounter is likewise bridal: it echoes the Song of Songs. Moreover the opening of Mary's question, 'Where...?' may be meant to evoke God's question in another garden—Eden. Throwing out another subtle hint about the reversal of the curse of sin and death, and a new Eve.

It's no coincidence Jesus' first miracle involves a Bride.

And water. Wine too—which, by the Gospel's finale, takes on a connotation of blood covenant.

Yet the miracle at Cana wasn't particularly special. It's simply, as CS Lewis indicated,[16] the same mystery occurring daily in grape-vines. God takes water, adds sunlight and minerals and voilà! With a little fermentation and aging, there's a fine vintage wine.

The miracle was in the timing: Jesus wasn't doing anything different from the Father; rather He was demonstrating His Lordship over time.

How do we participate with Him in this?

The answer is in the story of the wedding at Cana and also in the episode featuring Thomas, the skeptic who wouldn't believe unless he could see Jesus' wounds and touch His pierced side.

Even after coming to the same wondrous realisation as Nicodemus—that the new birth is through the wounded side of Christ—a reader of John's Gospel might still have wondered: how exactly do we enter that place to be born again?

By faith.

That's the message of Cana and the Upper Room.

Thomas exclaimed, 'My Lord and my God!' Mary simply told the servants at the wedding: 'Do whatever He tells you.'

That's faith.

When we do whatever Jesus tells us.

John, a witness at different times to Thomas' and Mary's words, summarises it all in his first epistle to the churches. He wraps up this connection between faith, water, blood and Spirit:

> *Who is it that overcomes the world? Only the one who believes that Jesus is the Son of God. This is the one who came by water and blood—Jesus Christ. He did not come by water only, but by water and blood. And it is the Spirit who testifies, because the Spirit is the truth. For there are three that testify: the Spirit, the water and the blood; and the three are in agreement.*
>
> 1 John 5:5–8 NIV

'Women were created from the rib of man to be beside him, not from his head to top him, nor from his feet to be trampled by him, but from under his arm to be protected by him, near to his heart to be loved by him.'

Matthew Henry, *An Exposition of the Old and New Testament*

The great weakness of English renditions of the Greek New Testament is the tendency to forget it is already a translation from Hebrew thought. In addition, there's an unvoiced assumption that a one-to-one correspondence of meaning exists between words in different languages.

Yet nothing could be further from the truth. Some languages have words for which there is no equivalent idea in any other tongue. Sometimes, to the great peril of the translator, the nearest word in the second language has unfortunate additional overtones. Such is the case when it comes to the Greek and Hebrew words for *submit*. Our English translations give Greek 'hupotasso' a connotation of being *pressed down*, however the Hebrew 'nasa'' means *to lift up*.

This has vast ramifications when it comes to the meaning of *submit* in Paul's exhortations: *'Everyone must submit himself to the governing authorities,'* (Romans 13:1 NIV) and *'Wives, submit to your husbands.'* (Ephesians 5:22; Colossians 3:18 NIV)

These ramifications have been explored at length in *God's Panoply*.[17] In a similar vein, it's worth examining the very last words of Jesus on the Cross.

John tells us that Jesus' last utterance was: *'It is finished.'* (John 19:30 NIV) Shortly afterwards His side was pierced with a lance and blood and water flowed out.

Brian Simmons points out that the original Aramaic Jesus would have used for *'It is finished'* would be 'kalah', *fulfilled, completed, brought to an end*. It is a homonym—that is, it sounds just like 'kallah', *bride*. So, what did Jesus actually say? 'Kalah' or 'kallah'? Which one did He actually mean?

Simmons, in *The Passion Translation*, encompasses both meanings and renders Jesus' final words as: 'It is finished, My Bride!'[18]

Yet it seems John has translated 'kalah' from Aramaic into Greek as if it has no double meaning—no wedding overtones whatever. If there was a connotation of *bride* in Jesus' words, why didn't John specifically mention it?

As a matter of fact, he did.

He contextualised it so that no first-century reader could miss the double meaning. We miss the nuptial allusion because, while we forensically scrutinise the meaning of Greek words in the text, we don't think about other elements just as important to literature in the ancient world. We don't have the integrated mindset of writers from past centuries. So we fail to examine the arithmetic design or look for poetic devices such as chiasmus to help us clarify the meaning of particular statements.

In the twenty-first century, western literary structure is all about rises and falls in the tension as a plot builds to a climax, before (hopefully) a swift wrap-up of all loose ends. But John was a Hebrew thinker, using—and incidentally revolutionising—Greek literary conventions. The structure of ancient narrative is nothing like that of modern novel.

John's contextualisation of Jesus' statement, 'It is finished,' uses chiasmus—the parallel imaging of ideas—at the back and front of His gospel. In fact, at least 22 mirror-pair elements exist, most of which use exactly the same names so they can be easily identified. Jesus' statement is, as we've already seen, followed by imagery of Eve and new birth. His dialogue with Mary Magdalene reflects the language used in the Song of Songs and, in the chiasmus, directly parallels the wedding feast at Cana.

Jesus' last words on the Cross show He was thinking of us. His bride.

As Simmons says: 'His cross fulfilled and finished the prophecies of the Messiah's first coming to the earth. There was nothing written that was not fulfilled and now offered to His bride.'[19]

The promises of Jesus to the new Eve are lavish and uncompromising, involving nothing less than the mending of the world.

It is not as a child that I believe and confess Jesus Christ. My hosanna is born of a furnace of doubt.

Fyodor Michailovitch Dostoevsky,
quoted by Harold Victor Martin in
Kierkegaard, the Melancholy Dane.

The twentieth century ushered in an era of impatience. We've got used to having everything instantly: from coffee to fast food to bank loan approvals. The culture is now all-pervasive. Even salvation, once a matter of anguished soul-searching and careful consideration of covenant obligations, is reduced to a formula. A presentation that could be easily compressed into five minutes, a prayer accomplished in just one. Some of these formulaic, prescription-like prayers do not mention repentance, some don't even mention Jesus![20]

God has undoubtedly worked through these methods, anyway. Despite their flaws and imperfections and, in some cases, outright heresy. He is, after all, God. But it would be presumptuous to think that everyone who has said a 'Sinner's Prayer' is born again. The early church tended to think that, like the first disciples of Jesus, it was a good idea to have three years of instruction in matters of faith. That aside, however, there's still an issue: the tendency in modern thinking to present the 'new birth' the wrong way around.

Kenneth Leech points out there's a power structure in the usual wording about inviting Jesus into your life or asking Him into your heart. The emphasis is not on Jesus, but rather on the individual seeking salvation. It's as if we're doing Jesus a favour: 'It sought to bring Jesus into our lives instead of bringing us into His. The gospel as preached in the west no longer helped to turn the world upside down but rather served to reinforce its false values and structures.'[21]

Instead it's more appropriate to recognise that Jesus is Lord and ask Him if He would invite us into the new birth—His life—through His pierced and wounded side. Sure enough, this is the prospective Bride proposing to the Bridegroom! But, take heart, He doesn't say 'no'!

Once we are in Him, having entered new life through His wounds, we are born again.

Once we are in Him, we are one with Him.

Once we are in Him, we have returned to oneness with God.

Once we are in Him, we are hidden from the enemy.

Once we are in Him, we are sons and daughters of the Father and can be trained to take up our inheritance.

We are, however, not instantly mature. We're infants who have said *'yes'* to God's request to re-form the broken pottery of our lives back into the whole of the original design. Where does He start with this process?

Anywhere, of course. He's not restricted.

However, generally speaking, whatever other aspect of our lives we might think needs works, there's one part we overlook. And that's the need to give Him permission to renovate our names.

If we've been addicted to anything—and that doesn't just mean alcohol or drugs, food, gambling, shopping, social media or pornography; far too many of us are people-pleasers and approval junkies—we've operated out of shame. Remember guilt is meant to drive us to seek God's forgiveness; but shame twists and distorts our very identity. It mangles our destiny.

And mutilates the source of them both: name.

We are so used to thinking of names as insignificant we don't see them as they really are: the fuse that empowers our existence, pushing us relentlessly out of a kernel of potential into an unimaginably glorious destiny.

3

Seams of Gold

GOD HAS, AS MENTIONED PREVIOUSLY, an exceedingly long nose. He revealed this to Moses one day on the enigmatic Mount Sinai. 'Enigmatic' because God's instructions about the mountain are a riddle at best. At times, no living creature—human or animal—was to approach it on pain of death. This ban seemed to be still in place when God invited seventy elders to dine with Him halfway up. Moses is told by God that no one can see His face and live, but the seventy elders, along with Moses and Aaron, thrive in God's presence.

It's all very mysterious.

And yet, at Sinai, we can find a prophetic foretaste of the new birth. Moses asks to see God's face, only to be told that it's too dangerous. But, God says, He will cause His glory to pass in front of Moses and will allow him to see His back. Positioning Moses in a cleft in the rock, God proclaimed:

'The Lord, the Lord, the compassionate and gracious God, slow to anger, abounding in love...'

Exodus 34:6 NIV

The Rock, as we learn in 1 Corinthians 10:4, is Jesus. The cleft in the Rock, like the wound in the side of Jesus, is the only true refuge in times of trouble. Hidden in Christ, we are safe from the judgment of the Holy One, the schemes of the Enemy, the temptations of the flesh.

But, like Moses, we have to ask.

And our request should conform to Kenneth Leech's insight: not that Jesus should come into our hearts and lives, but that we should be placed within His life, close to His heart, deep in His wounded side.

As God placed Moses in the cleft in the Rock, so we should ask to be placed in the side of Jesus. To do otherwise is to reverse the Bride with her Husband and Maker; to mutilate the very concept of who we are—to disfigure our identity and, with it, our destiny and our names.

Names capture events, encase reputations, and encapsulate entire networks of ideas. ...When God revealed his name to Moses, he was in effect saying that from Egypt on, when Israel heard and used his name they should understand that its meaning should be filled with the knowledge of his acts in delivering them from Egypt.

Andrew Reid, *Exodus: Saved for Service*

Along with the mutilation of our names, mutilation frequently occurs to the concept of gender. It's time to wake up to the union of masculine and feminine overlooked in many translations.

The hallmark of the kingdom of heaven is courtesy. Some people may dispute that notion, on the basis of Jesus' words in Matthew 11:12 NKJV:

'*From the days of John the Baptist until now the kingdom of heaven suffers violence, and the violent take it by force.*'

John Klein and Adam Spears in their superb book, *Lost in Translation*, suggest this is far from an accurate rendering. Rather, it should be more like: '*From the days of John the Baptist until now the kingdom of heaven has been bursting forth, and (we of) the advance guard possess its full force.'*

Hardly the aggressive stance recommended in so many other versions. More sensible in context, too.

While we're here, let me raise an overlooked problem in western Christianity: we're apt to accept a culture of violence so extreme we don't even realise how desensitised we've become.[22] We deplore bad language and abhor any gratuitous sexual presentation in literature, film or art. But we allow brutality and cruelty a free pass without even recognising it.

Worse still, we unthinkingly take mental strongholds which tolerate violence into the study of Scripture. It's not entirely our fault. Translators impose their biases on the text and, for the most part, we are reliant on the work of flawed, prejudiced human beings.

Even the title we commonly use to describe God reflects the agenda of the man who commissioned the King James Version. A lord is not as high as a king. 'King God' might seem gauche by comparison with 'Lord God', but only because it's unfamiliar. Such is the ongoing influence of James' fervent belief in the divine right of kings.

Don't get me wrong. I have an extremely high view of Scripture. I believe it is the infallible Word of God. But this doesn't mean I trust *any* English translation without reservation.

I nevertheless believe God can do a perfect work, even through perilously imperfect translations.

However, there's still an issue regarding violence: in a culture where aggression is the 'strong' response and peaceableness the 'weaker', academic translators tend to choose alternatives perceived as physically robust, not spiritually so.

Thus, who is likely to see, as I have mentioned in *God's Panoply*, that the Armour of God is about a divine kiss? And that God's kiss is our covenantal protection?

Or who is likely to realise that, behind the studied military overtones of Paul's command, *'Wives, submit to your husbands,'* there's some subtle

Hebrew poetry also related to kissing? Who is going to audaciously render it as it was undoubtedly intended to be understood: 'Wives, lift up your husbands; be their companions for battle'?

Or who is likely to notice, as I have indicated in *God's Pageantry*, the allusions to seven flowers in the Armour of God passage? Or indicate it has a musical setting? Or point out that it is underpinned by the mathematics of covenant?

Who is likely to suspect the prevalence of our violent mindset is so culturally widespread it would be easy to overlook an alternative translation to '*The Lord is a man of war; the Lord is His name*,' in Exodus 15:3?

Admittedly, in the context of the celebration song after the crossing of the Red Sea, 'man of war' is likely. However, that doesn't preclude the possibility the verse *also* means: '*The Lord is a man of bread; the Lord is His name*.'

The words for *bread* and *war* in Hebrew are the same, just as the words for *putting on armour* and *kissing* are identical. Significantly this means that Bethlehem, *house of bread*, is also *house of warfare*.

This, in fact, explains why the history of Bethlehem is one where the actions of individuals precipitate widespread bloodshed. One of the most gruesome stories in Scripture involves a priest retrieving his concubine from Bethlehem. Judges 19–20 shows threshold covenant violation resulting in gang rape, progressing to tribal conflict and ultimately genocide. In later centuries, Bethlehem was again associated with bloodshed when Herod issued orders to kill every boy under two. In recent times, the Crimean War began over the dispute between Greek Orthodox priests and their Latin Catholic counterparts over the keys to the Church of the Nativity in Bethlehem.

Names encode destiny. When the history of a place does not align with the meaning of its name, then it's appropriate to look deeper. Thus to take another example: Jerusalem is hardly the city of peace its name proclaims but conforms far more to its earlier name, Jebus, *pain*, *persecution* and *walled in*.

To return to the Lord as a *man of bread*—a provider, a sustainer—this title alludes to the story of Abraham and Jehovah Jireh, *the Lord will provide*. It provides a historic backdrop of God's unchangeable determination to redeem the firstborn and bring them to Himself. It also speaks volumes about the everlasting immutability of God's character by evoking the name God revealed to Abram as they undertook their second covenant with each other. It harks back to El Shaddai, *the strong-breasted one*, with all its overtones of sustenance and nurture.

'So God created mankind... in the image of God He created them; male and female He created them.'

Genesis 1:27 NIV

The tendency to overlook the feminine aspects in the image of God is, in my view, the greatest challenge for translators. Sure, on the masculine side in Exodus 15:3, we have the Divine Warrior defending His people. But enfolded with this is a feminine aspect: Provider of Bread. (And if you harbour doubts that image is culturally feminine, may I point out the word 'lady' ultimately derives from *bread-giver*?)

Perhaps we could see the God described in the Exodus as a lot like a mother hen, gathering her chicks under her wings, flapping them ahead of her as she stands between them and the implacable menace determined to devour them.

In presenting God from Genesis to Malachi as hyper-masculine, translators do us a disservice. Jesus looks gentler and more inclusive. He chose a woman as his first evangelist; women as the first witnesses to His resurrection; gave way to a woman's pleas when it came to his first miracle.

Yet He is the Bridegroom and the entire assembly of the church—every man or woman who has experienced the 'new birth'—are all the Bride in relation to Him.

It's far too easy to think of Jesus in diametric contrast to the Father. When He repeatedly said that They are One.

...once in Israel, love came to us incarnate and stood in the doorway between two worlds, and we were all afraid.

Annie Dillard

Jesus performed His first miracle at a wedding feast in Cana, encouraged by the faith and intervention of His mother. The structural chiasmus of John's gospel parallels two bridal moments: this one with His mother and the post-resurrection scene in the garden with another Mary.

His interaction with Mary Magdalene is not meant to be understood by itself. The dialogue alludes to the bridal interchange in Song of Songs and reflects the question of God to Adam in Eden. Yet its most immediate context is, in the light of John's careful book-ending, the wedding at Cana.

There Jesus directs the servants to draw water to fill six large earthenware jars. When the steward tastes the contents of these pottery jars, he calls the bridegroom and explains that most people leave the inferior wine until last. Until, it's implied, the guests are tipsy and their discernment compromised. But, the steward exclaims, in this case the best wine has been reserved until last.

John has kept a careful chronology up to this point in his gospel. Although some commentators take his precise indication of 'the third day' as simply meaning Tuesday, the third day of the Jewish week, I read it as six days since the start of his narrative. And this is a very suggestive number. Many writers also note that 'six is the number for man' when, in fact, 666 is more accurately 'the number of *a* man'. Six is not always to do with humanity—and this instance is a case in point.

If this chronology does refer to a time lapse of six days, it not only suggests a threshold covenant is taking place, it alludes to a specific calendar date. It suggests the wedding occurred on the feast of Sukkot, the seventh and last festival of the Jewish year, a celebration originally associated with gathering into storage of grain and new wine.[23]

Perfect. Jesus creates new wine and allows others to gather it in on the ordained day for such activity.

Now, by back-calculation, we can determine that John's narrative starts on the feast of Yom Kippur, the day of atonement. John is asked by the Jewish leaders who he is. Exactly two years later, on the day of atonement, Jesus would ask a similar question of His disciples: 'Who do men say that I am?' And six days after that momentous question, He took three of them up a high mountain to witness an exposition of His glory. The threshold markers leading up to Jesus' transfiguration with their two dozen parallels to Abraham's second and third covenants with God are detailed at length in *God's Pageantry*.

Even without the likelihood that the wedding feast occurred at Sukkot, it bears many hallmarks of a threshold event:

- a first time
- an emergence into the light of destiny
- an unveiling of identity
- a covenant
- a negotiation
- a sacrifice

A first time: Jesus has never performed a public miracle before.

An emergence: everything will change for Jesus when word of the miracle gets around.

An unveiling: until the miracle, Jesus is just another itinerant rabbi but afterwards, huge questions hang over His identity.

A covenant: it's at a wedding, where two are becoming one, and it's using wine—later to become symbolic of His blood. Thus echoes of blood covenant exist here.

A negotiation: the first recorded threshold covenant between God and man was that with Abraham; following it, Abraham negotiates with God over the destruction of Sodom. Just so, Mary negotiates with Jesus about providing wine for the wedding.

A sacrifice: Jesus is hesitant; He equivocates as He speaks to His mother, reluctant to commit to this miracle seemingly out of the right timing for His declaration of His power.

Ironically, everything about this miracle hinges on timing. There's nothing out of the ordinary about water becoming wine. As we've already noted, CS Lewis pointed out that this change happens whenever water, sunlight and minerals are reconfigured by the process of photosynthesis and turned into grapes which are the basis of wine.

In this instance, Jesus uses water, the minerals of clay jars and the Light of the World to create a superior wine. He does not do anything that the Father does not do on a daily basis within a grape-vine. He later said, '*I only do the works I see the Father doing, for the Son does the same works as His Father.*' (John 5:19 TPT)

The miracle is all in the timing. Jesus shows Himself to be the Lord of time. He is therefore the creator of day and night, of dark and light, of the world and all that is in it.

Brian Simmons relates the six clay jars to humanity. He makes the connection through six, using the common assumption it is the 'number of man'. However, I believe six is a reference to the threshold covenant—the clay jars, in and of themselves, representing humanity. After all Adam, as our prototype, was made from earth. There are also sufficient reminders that we are clay and God is the Master Potter in the prophecies of Isaiah and Jeremiah not to have to fall back on 'number of man' as the explanation.

Simmons, however, has a beautiful and perceptive thought about the contents of the clay pots. Man's method of helping others is nothing but water. But when the Spirit of Jesus dwells within our clay, we bring limitless joy to the world.

Max Lucado points out that, when a potter fires a clay vessel, he checks its readiness by pulling it out of the furnace and thumping it. If it 'sings' it's ready. But if it 'thuds' it has to be put back in. *'Count it all joy when you fall into various trials... the testing of your faith produces patience,'* he says, quoting James 1:2 NKJV as he refers to a variety of the thumps of life: flat tyres, burnt meals, traffic jams, long queues, grouchy colleagues, impossible deadlines, dirty clothes on the floor.

None of these things is big enough to be a crisis but enough of them can trigger a violent over-reaction. 'Character,' says Lucado, 'is checked by thumping.'

After being in the furnace for a while, what do our clay vessels of self do when they're thumped? Sing or thud?

If you're like me, it'll be a tendency to thud first. And eventually—after a very long time—remember that I'm supposed to be singing.

Thanking God, praising Him—half-heartedly at first, I admit, but there's no point in not being genuine with God. He doesn't want false attitudes. He wants us to begin honestly, in dialogue with Him, so He can come down to inhabit even the tiniest mote of praise. And move on from there to swell our entire being with the new wine of His presence, overflowing out into the world.

However, let's not forget in this prolonged image of pots in the hands of the Potter, one of the profound mysteries of heaven: that God's pottery is also His poetry.

For we are His workmanship, created in Christ Jesus for good works, which God prepared beforehand that we should walk in them.

Ephesians 2:10 NKJV

The Greek word which is translated *workmanship* comes from 'poeo', *poem*.

As I have reiterated so often in *God's Poetry*, we are divine poems. But we are also His pottery.

He is both Author and Potter and, in heavenly terms, there is no distinction between the two.

The poem is the pot and the pot the poem and both come into being through His divine whisper of a name.

Does the clay dispute with the one who shapes it, saying, 'Stop, you're doing it wrong!' Does the pot exclaim, 'How clumsy can you be?'

Isaiah 45:9 NLT

For some of us, our clay pot is broken. Seriously so. The traumas of life have been so severe that there's no possibility of thudding, let alone of singing. We've been shattered, spoiled, damaged. Our personalities are fragmented and dissociated, without any hope of wholeness. Years of counselling has made some difference, even significant difference—but, at the rate we're going, the fullness of life that Jesus promised to His followers will always elude us.

For those of us in this situation, dealing with ungodly covenants is an essential key. Holding out a hand in faith, and asking God to gather all the pieces of ourselves into it, drop them into it and then handing them to Him for repair, may be the beginning of restoration.

And, indeed, it's true in instances like this that perhaps His repair will always show the cracks. That the mending won't be as exceptional and invisible as the work on the terracotta warriors of Mount Li.

Instead it may be like Kintsugi work—the elegant and beautiful Japanese art of joining broken pottery with seams of gold. Like the craftsman who sees the breakage and repair of a pot as part of its history, rather than a set of cracks to disguise, the Master Potter may display His work of salvation in us through exquisite golden seams.

Like the woman who'd had seven demons and who broke an

alabaster jar to allow its contents to anoint the feet of Jesus, so the Holy Spirit in us is not limited by our wholeness or brokenness—we too are called to a consecrated work: to minister to God.

As we praise and glorify Him, He comes to inhabit our praises. As we lift His name, He creates those seams of gold joining our scattered fragments of self together again.

God takes life's broken pieces and gives us unbroken peace.

Wilbert Donald Gough

The story of a woman anointing the feet of Jesus with a rare and costly ointment is told in three of the four gospels. Each account reveals something slightly different. Mark tells us it happened in Bethany at the house of Simon, a man who had been healed of leprosy by Jesus, and that, straight afterwards, Judas Iscariot went off to betray Jesus.[24] Luke adds that Simon was a Pharisee. Surprisingly, given that Luke was a doctor, he doesn't reveal Simon's medical condition. But he does reveal that Jesus discerned Simon's thoughts about the woman's unsavoury reputation and told him a pointed parable.[25]

John adds that the incident occurred six days before the Passover, gives us the woman's name and notes that Judas Iscariot protested the waste of the ointment for underhanded motives.[26]

Now at the end of his gospel John reveals this:

'Jesus did many other things as well. If every one of them were written down... the whole world would not have room for the books that would be written.'

John 21:25 NIV

So why choose a well-known story that two other writers have already told in detail? What did the other stories miss that was so significant John felt it necessary to revisit the same scene with additional information?

Perhaps it's the fact the event occurred six days before the Passover. (Mark makes the confusing statement it happened two days away from the Feast of Unleavened Bread and the Passover, as if they were the same event. John seems to be correcting the ambiguity in Mark's testimony.)

Six days before the Passover. That's flagging far more than a precise date. The Passover is a celebration and commemoration of the first threshold covenant between God and the Jewish people. It's an archetype of all threshold events.

In Scripture, it's common to find a name covenant taking place six days before a threshold covenant. An example is Jesus exchanging names with Simon[27] and calling him Peter, then six days later taking him up a mountain for a threshold covenant.

Is John therefore telling us that Jesus did the same for a woman as He did for a man? That there is, as Paul had written and John was now reinforcing by narrating this specific example, no distinction between male and female, just as there was none between Jew and Greek, slave and free?

If this were so, we would have to find the woman identified and we would have to find other subtle aspects of naming in what happens. And of course this is precisely what happens.

Mary opened an alabaster jar of a precious and expensive ointment imported from India—spikenard—to the consternation of at least two witnesses. As the perfume filled the room, Jesus defended Mary against the words of Judas Iscariot and the thoughts of the host, Simon.

The word used for *perfume* in the Greek text is myrrh. A valuable secretion of a gnarled arid-landscape tree, myrrh forms tear-like pearls and has been used for cosmetic treatments since at least the time of Queen Esther. It was one of the gifts given to Jesus as a baby by the Magi.

It was commonly associated with anointing the bridegroom.

Myrrh, which in Hebrew is 'more', happens to be related to Mary's name. Mary comes from Miriam, containing 'mar', *bitter*. Miriam also contains 'yam', *sea*—thus we derive words like *marine* and *marinade* from it. Since tears are like salty water and are often the result of bitter circumstances, 'mar' can be used figuratively of *crying*.

Mary comes to Jesus and, through perfume and tears, offers Him her name. He accepts her sacrifice and becomes her covenant defender. To complete the work, she'd have to be present six days later at a threshold covenant.

Although many scholars believe Mary of Bethany and Mary Magdalene are two separate individuals, I consider that John leaves us sufficient information to say they are the same. There's no point in a name covenant without a threshold covenant six days later—and, as close as possible to the right time, given Jesus' death in the interim—Mary Magdalene was there just after the resurrection.

As Peter, James and John were witnesses for the threshold event of the Transfiguration, Mary witnesses the most awesome threshold event of all time: the resurrection of the firstborn son of God from the dead. She becomes, as Augustine later said, the 'Apostle to the Apostles'.

When we look at all three Gospel accounts of Mary pouring oil over Jesus' head and feet, we discover the depth of Hebrew poetry hidden in the scene:

- mar, *crying*
- mar, *drop, flowing down*
- more, *myrrh*
- merqach, *perfume*
- merqachach, *pot of ointment*
- mirzach, *banquet*
- marach, *rub*
- marat, *polish; plucked off hair*
- margalah, *feet; at the place of the feet*
- mara', *filthy*

- mara', *lift up*
- mara', *bitterness*
- mirmac, *trampling place*
- mara'ashah, *at his head*
- maruwq, *purification, bodily rubbing*[28]
- mirsha'ath, *wicked woman*
- mirmah, *treachery, fraud*
- mera', *mischief*
- merea', *confidential friend*
- mare' (Aramaic), *lord*

All of these are head rhymes for Mary. And all of them are either used in the text or alluded to indirectly.

If there is any doubt this is a name covenant, with all of these massive poetic overtones, let it be dispelled by the oil. In Hebrew this is 'shemen'—which like 'nashamah', *breath*, 'neshama', *soul* and ''asham', *guilt*—contains the word 'shem', *name*. We could perhaps even boldly translate 'shemen', *oil*, as *new name, regeneration of name, renewal of name*.

Since naming is the breath of life, perhaps anointing oil for the healing of the sick should be seen as more than simply symbolic of renewing name and therefore restoring life. In fact, Paul uses the notion of perfumed oil in this sense:

'We are... the aroma of Christ among those who are being saved, and those who are perishing. To one we are an aroma that brings death; to the other, an aroma that brings life...'

2 Corinthians 2:15–16 NIV

Here he refers to the way the Roman armies celebrated their victories. As well as parading their defeated enemies through the streets in chains, they burned incense on altars throughout the city. Even those who missed seeing the procession couldn't miss the aroma of victory.

Mary Magdalene rubbed Jesus' feet with the aroma of victory. The scent of a king would have been all over His clothes—even up to His crucifixion.

This is a very different kind of name covenant to those undertaken by men in the Scriptures. Abram, Jacob, Simon—they all waited for God to take the initiative. But here a woman steps out.

It's not the first time in Scripture that has happened.

We have become God's poetry, a re-created people that will fulfil the destiny He has given each one of us, for we are joined to Jesus, the Anointed One. Even before we were born, God planned in advance our destiny and the good works we would do to fulfil it.

Ephesians 2:10 TPT

At the beginning of Genesis, the presence of God is inescapable, but at the beginning of Exodus, He isn't mentioned at all. Andrew Reid says: '...in the absence of God, five women make their presence known... If there are heroes in the text, it is these, for they act to preserve God's future for His people through protecting male children in general and Moses in particular.'[29]

Jewish rabbis have repeatedly noted nuances in the Hebrew Scriptures that are universally ignored in Christian translations. Many of these affect the role of women. Yechiel Eckstein mentions a crucial detail left out of the following rendering:

'All who were willing, men and women alike, came and brought gold jewelry of all kinds: brooches, earrings, rings and ornaments. They all presented their gold as a wave offering to the Lord.'

Exodus 35:22 NIV

In Hebrew, the verse more literally reads: '*The men came on the heels of the women and brought gold jewelry of all kinds...*'[30]

The immense significance of this becomes even clearer when the incident of the golden calf is examined. Jewish sages recognise that, hidden in the pronouns, is a statement about the faithfulness of the mothers of Israel. Aaron had told the men to ask everyone for gold—their wives, their sons, their daughters. However, they got no jewelry from the women, a point completely occluded in over fifty Christian translations I've consulted.

These same women who refused to surrender their gold ornaments to be melted down for the golden calf were first in line to offer them for God's tabernacle. They also handed over the brass mirrors they'd been given by the Egyptian women to be reforged into the vast laver, the washing basin, for the Tabernacle entrance.

'When Moses finished setting up the tabernacle, he anointed and consecrated it and all its furnishings. He also anointed and consecrated the altar and all its utensils.'

Numbers 7:1 NKJV

Eckstein comments on this verse: 'the word chosen by Scripture for *finished*, "kalot", can also mean *bride*. One reason for the allusion to a bride at this juncture in time is because the children of Israel were the bride and God the groom; the completed Tabernacle would be their shared home. However, there is another significance to this word with a double meaning. While "kalot" describes an ending, it also points to a beginning. A bride is a symbol of a new beginning as a woman begins a new life with her marriage. The word "kalot", with its opposite connotations, teaches us that every end is also a beginning.'[31]

Here in this verse, we already have a foretaste of what it would mean for Jesus to finish His work of redemption and become the firstfruits of those to be resurrected.

Here also in this verse we see the consequences of the mothers of Israel remaining steadfast, while the men continually wavered. The completion of the Tabernacle paved the way for a new beginning. The women's faithfulness made a difference time after time. According to various Jewish commentators, they were the first to agree to the covenant of the Law. God treated them differently: he instructed Moses to speak to women with gentle encouragement and to men with stern admonition.[32]

The incident with the golden calf was a point of no return in society as well as domestic relationships for the Israelites. Huge and permanent changes resulted. Ordinary men lost their position as priests in their own households—a privilege given to the Levites when they heeded the call of Moses to side with God.[33]

On the one hand, while the men lost substantial rights, the women received a reward. Although this gift is not recorded in Scripture, it is mentioned in Jewish commentaries. In Judaism, a once-a-month holiday exists specifically for women. Their actions at Mount Sinai are cited as the reason for its institution. Not just once, but at least three times, they remained steadfast when the men fell away.

So every New Moon, women have been granted a day off as an ongoing memorial to commemorate their faithfulness to God.

Jewish commentary also points out that, when Numbers 26:64–65 speaks of an entire generation who died in the Desert of Sinai, this specifically refers to the men—excepting Caleb and Joshua—and not to the women. Yechiel Eckstein, yet again, refers us to the original Hebrew, indicating that the verse reads: 'not one *man* was left...'

'Why didn't the women die in the desert as the men did?' he asks. 'Is it because God took pity on the women over the men? Not at all. The sages teach that the men had lost their faith on that dreadful night when the spies spoke negatively about the land of Israel—but the women did not. They kept their faith. Even though the spies had reported enemies of large proportions, well-fortified cities, and a land that swallowed its people, the women closed their ears to the men's words. Instead, they opened their hearts to the word of God, who had promised to lead them into a good land. They had passed the test of faith.'[34]

Jewish thought again and again celebrates the achievements and faithfulness of women. What on earth happened to Christian thought that no translation of Scripture even hints at this monumental role in salvation history?

Said the robin to the sparrow, 'I should really like to know,
why these anxious human beings rush around and worry so.'
Said the sparrow to the robin, 'Friend, I think that it must be,
that they have no Heavenly Father such as cares for you and me.'

Elizabeth Cheney

As a result of the golden calf incident, ordinary men lost the right to be priests in their own household. Levites were excepted, because they sided with Moses when he called for the people to come back to God. This right was eventually restored through the work of Jesus. But it was no longer exclusive to men. All believers were invited to share in Jesus' priestly work.

This is not to suggest all Jewish men were as inclusive as Jesus. Many were as misogynist as the Greeks.

Five hundred years before Christ, Pythagoras had devised a number system consisting of masculine and feminine numbers: the male ones were good, the female ones evil. As Margaret Wertheim has pointed out in her superb analysis, *Pythagoras' Trousers*, Christianity has been vastly more influenced by Pythagoras and its ally, Platonism, than we can ever begin to imagine.

Through centuries of theology aligned with Greek thinking rather than Hebrew, we bring presuppositions to Bible translation that rupture the seamless witness of the New and Old Testaments.

We relegate women to second place. Some denominations restrict the priesthood to men and, even amongst those that don't, the average conference line-up reveals the hidden truth. When there's not a single woman amongst a dozen featured speakers, the real attitude is obvious.

The church is quite overt about this, society at large more subtle.

I used to teach mathematics in a large provincial school with a tough reputation. A group of university researchers arrived to assess the attitude of the girls towards the sciences. After a couple of days, they were scratching their heads as they came into the staffroom for morning tea. One confided: 'We may need to stay a week longer. So far we're getting really skewed results.'

'In what way?' our Head of Department asked.

'Every single girl we've interviewed is incredibly positive about mathematics and science as a future option. Even if they're not considering it personally, they don't hate the prospect. The results are in complete opposition to every other school we've been in.'

Our staff laughed, pleased.

'Look around,' I said. 'Take a close look at each member of staff.'

The researchers looked but still didn't get it.

'This is not a top school. The reason we have a gender imbalance of fourteen females to one male in this staffroom—with a consequent flow-on positive attitude of girls to science—is that men make it clear they'll resign rather than come here.' I didn't mention we'd had one guy so appalled after a single morning teaching chemistry, he'd applied enough pressure in the right places to get transferred within forty-eight hours to the most prestigious school in the state. 'Bet you if you interviewed the boys in this school they'd see science as a woman's profession.'

The researchers took a collective deep breath. 'They do,' one of them said.

They'd left by lunch time.

Gordon Dalbey points out, regarding racial equality, that 'historically, whites have granted others a rung on the national level of esteem only after exploiting it themselves and then scorning it as lower.'[35] In practice this means that Afro-American women were only allowed as Miss America contestants at the time the women's liberation pickets began. It also means that an integrated military came at the same time as the anti-war movement. Despite the seeming advances, despite the apparent change in societal attitudes, the deeper reality is that the doors of 'equality' only open when what was once prized is now despised.

Just so, it's only when the priesthood comes to be devalued that a way opens for women to become pastors, ministers and clergy. It's not so much about allowing women access to the office but about how tarnished the position is in the eyes of men.

Margaret Wertheim posits that the imbalance of the two genders in physics reflects that in the church. And that she traces, not to Jewish religious belief, but rather to Greek philosophy and Pythagorean mysticism.

The problem with having a skewed view of the value of the feminine—or the masculine—is simple. We are perpetuating the separation of man and woman that occurred at the Fall. Instead of embracing the covenantal oneness of the Bride with her Redeemer.

'You have listened to fears, child,' said Aslan. 'Come, let me breathe on you. Forget them. Are you brave again?'

CS Lewis, Prince Caspian

My mum has a trick question she uses when she's counselling women. It's this: 'Can you finish this statement with the first thing that comes to mind? "Men are————"'

She's heard it all. Every shade and nuance of dishonour.

Much of it is deserved. But we still reap what we sow. Dishonour breeds dishonour breeds dishonour.

Meanwhile we all crave honour.

Maybe I shouldn't say *'we all'*—it's unwise to attribute my besetting addiction to everyone else. I've told the story (twice) in previous books in this series how I discovered that the virtue leading me ever so subtly away from God was a love of truth and a desire to both give and receive honour. So I won't tell it again, other than to say it surfaced as I was investigating the name 'Melissa'.[36]

For some people it's really difficult to comprehend that the most insidious idols we can create for ourselves are addictive virtues. We can too easily turn 'God is love' into 'Love is god' and run the risk of deifying a feeling of affection or even lust. We can twist 'God is peace' into 'Peace is god' and wind up appeasing evil. We can take 'God is just', flip it to 'Justice is god' and revisit the cruel judgmentalism of centuries past. Or start with 'God is merciful', spin it until it reads, 'Mercy is god' and decide that reconciliation with Him is simply a matter of divine grace and forgiveness. The part of the reconciliation equation involving human repentance is forgotten.

Any virtue, pursued to an extreme at the exclusion of all others, is deadly.

Recently this point came up while several friends and I happened to be discussing the Battle of Maldon. A thousand years ago or so, a horde of marauding Vikings clashed with a troop of local defenders in a town on the Essex coast. Maldon is remembered, when more strategic skirmishes have been forgotten, because this particular conflict was immortalised in a poem. Only a fragment is left but it's enough. A line from its powerful finale is still stirring even a millennium later.

The locals predictably lost, despite their heroic virtue. For many years, the valiant last stand of the lord-protector's thanes was seen to embody the ideal of nobility in Dark Age warfare. The words of an old retainer defending the dead body of his lord echo down the centuries:

Will shall be the sterner,
heart the bolder,
spirit the greater,
as our strength lessens.

Heroic as this may be, JRR Tolkien called a significant aspect of the poem's interpretation into question with his doubts about a key word: ofermōd. This word is used to describe Byrhtnoth, lord-protector of Maldon, as he nobly agrees to a request of the Vikings to move to ground more advantageous to them.

Tolkien theorised it was a mistake to consider the use of ofermōd signified praise of Byrhtnoth. Literally meaning *over-heart*, ofermōd's modern translation as *greatness of heart*, *overboldness* or *excessive honour* might just disguise a dark underbelly. Because, as Tolkien said, ofermōd was rare and was also used in contemporary medieval verse to describe Lucifer, he suggested it could indicate a thread of devilish pride woven into the cloth of chivalry making up the lord-protector's honour.

Thinking of my own experience when God indicated that honour was in danger of becoming an idol, it occurred to me during our discussion of the Battle of Maldon that virtue can be infiltrated by vice—honour, for example, can reach stupid heights. Pride can hide behind principle, influencing decisions that place people in harm's way.

The father in the story of the Prodigal Son does not esteem honour so highly that he is not prepared to sacrifice it to spare his son shame. Likewise Jesus did not spare Himself shame and was not afraid to sacrifice His honour and His place in heaven for the sake of others.

That's the balance we need: to esteem honour but not so highly that it becomes god. And because humans are inveterate idol-makers, there's another thing to watch out for once we achieve such a balance.

That Balance, in its own turn, does not become god.

I love the name of honour more than I fear death.

William Shakespeare, *Julius Caesar*

Once honour and Lucifer occur in the same sentence, some uneasy questions start to raise their voices and beg to be answered. It's always intrigued me that God created everything good. Not just good but very good. *Perfect.*

Yet somehow, one day, imperfection is found in the most stunningly beautiful work: the anointed cherub we call Lucifer. If you've noticed I've used the phrase 'we call Lucifer' in a way that suggests Lucifer is not actually his name, you'd be right. But for the moment, let's keep using the common term.

One day—almost it seems out of the blue—this cherub who was so lovely God Himself described him in Ezekiel 28:12 as 'a model of perfection, full of wisdom and perfect in beauty' was found to harbour pride. How is this even possible? If the perfection didn't save him from corruption, why didn't the wisdom? Or vice versa?

Could it be this pride grew out of ofermōd, just as medieval people thought? Was it originally about an excessive emphasis on honour?

It was the role of the cherubim to ensure that only unblemished honour and unsullied righteousness—perfect sinlessness, utter holiness—approached God's throne. As an anointed guardian and covering cherub, this was part of Lucifer's office. When it came to choosing, did Lucifer place Honour in a higher position than God Himself? Did he value his job more than the One who gave him the job?

God, in the person of Jesus, was willing to give up honour and take on every aspect of shame imaginable. From a seemingly illegitimate birth to the humiliations of the cross, He emptied Himself of glory and exposed Himself to shame. All to take away our shame.

Yet Lucifer wants to project shame on to us, toxic shame that binds us in cords of hidden pride. He never wants shame taken away.

Because, if we lost our shame through the power of Jesus' blood, we'd get back our identities, our destinies and our names.

Through naming comes knowing.

Rainer Maria Rilke

The reason Lucifer wants to keep our names—quite apart from the astonishing power bound up in them—is that he doesn't have one of his own. This might seem surprising since Isaiah 14 apparently offers significant information on just that matter. However a name for the leader of the fallen angels actually isn't given. Ezekiel doesn't mention a name either, despite offering a wealth of detail in chapter 28 about his former role: an anointed cherub gorgeously apparelled in the finest gemstones, able to walk in and out amongst the stones of fire, a trader without peer.

The fact is, strictly speaking, Lucifer is not a name. Neither is Satan. The word 'Satan' actually comes from a Hebrew title and means *the adversary* or *the enemy*. Perhaps we'd be better using the more accurate terminology '*the* satan'.

In addition, the fallen angel we refer to as Lucifer may not be identical with the satan, even though we tend to use the words interchangeably. So transposable are these 'names' Lucifer and Satan in our thinking that even someone as careful in language and skilled in philology as JRR Tolkien mixed them up.

When he was discussing *The Battle of Maldon*, he drew attention to a connection between Lucifer and ofermōd in other old English poetry—

but, as it happens, this link never actually occurs. In early medieval literature, the Hebrew-inspired term 'Satan' or else an unnamed fallen angel was always coupled with ofermōd.

It was only in the seventeenth century that English translators created the name Lucifer[37] from another title, 'son of the morning', in Isaiah 14:12. It's been in common usage ever since.

Now, by naming, we offer immense power. We prophetically speak out an individual's unique identity and destiny within the corporate community.

This raises a terrible prospect. Have we returned to the satan the power of name?

The satan has a colleague who doesn't have a name either: Abaddon, the angel of death. Abaddon is a title meaning *the abyss*.

Why is it the chiefs of the fallen angels don't have names? How did the name Lucifer disguise this fact? And which of the two fallen cherubim has come to acquire this name bestowed by mankind? Is it the satan or is it Death?

Ravi Zacharias in *Why Jesus?* tells the story of a mentally impaired boy who lived in an Indian orphanage for the disabled. Because of the severity of his problems, he was always overlooked whenever a child was chosen for adoption. Gradually he fell into deep sadness—even with a vastly reduced mental capacity he was able to recognise he was the one always left behind. One day, an American couple who had adopted one of his friends rang to see if he was still there. The formal paperwork took many months but, as the day approached, the boy was told he would receive a new name when he went to America. Anson Josiah. AJ for short. From that point on, he would strut around the orphanage with a smile and tell everyone as he tapped himself on the chest: 'My name is AJ. You can call me AJ.'

Despite his impairment, he'd picked up what a name meant: belonging.

When you don't have a name, you don't belong.

The satan doesn't have a name. Neither does the Angel of Death.

There's an implication that God stripped it from the anointed cherub described in Ezekiel 28.

This is not quite the non-existence some of the Pharaohs tried to impose on their hated predecessors by removing every cartouche bearing their names, but it comes close. In having no name, only titles, the fallen cherubim have no identity, no calling. That's another reason they want to steal ours.

Why did God take away their names? I think the answer is given in the text: because of the vast extent and nature of their trade. The root for *trader* is also the root for *slander* and for *gossip*—both of which involve destroying names and reputations.

My view is that the fallen cherubim were trading names and the staggering power that's inherent in them. They stole and bargained with identities and destinies. We reap what we sow. That's an immutable law of the universe often expressed scientifically as: 'To every action, there is an equal and opposite reaction.'

The satan and his colleague, the Angel of Death, were stripped of their names because they were trading names.

And that's what the cherubim of the dark threshold still want: your name. Your identity, your destiny.

And it's why, in Scripture, you'll so often find name covenants linked to threshold covenants, and separated by six days.

4

Trading in Names

IN TRADITIONAL CHINESE CULTURE, it's considered very bad luck to name a child before birth. An unborn baby may be given a *milk name*—a false name—to confuse evil spirits.[38] This may persist into childhood. A boy may be given a plain or meaningless name to protect him. Sometimes even one of the opposite gender.

Bruce Lee, for instance, was always called by a girl's name, Sai Fon, *small phoenix*, even though his real name was *little dragon*. According to Bruce's wife, Linda, in the biography, *The Bruce Lee Story*: 'Mr. and Mrs. Lee had lost their first son, and according to Chinese tradition when future sons are born, they are often addressed by a girl's name in order to confuse the spirits who might steal away their souls.'[39]

The Chinese are not the only ones to exercise extreme care about revealing the names of cherished newborn children. In devout Jewish homes, the name of the child will never be spoken aloud until the time of circumcision for a boy or dedication for a girl. This precaution is taken to protect the baby from the predatory spirit known as Lilith. For fear that this 'Howling One', a demon of nightmare and vampirism, will come and murder the child, orthodox Jews will also place an amulet above the baby's crib inscribed with the names of three legendary angels.[40]

Conversely, some Chinese parents call their unwanted girls by boys' names with the intent of killing them. The girl is deliberately loaded with a portentous male name in order to draw the attention of a Lilith-like demon.

It's all too easy to think of this as superstitious nonsense. William Schnoebelen however notes that a superstitious practice can come, over a period of time, to be empowered by demonic forces. The occult term, 'egregore', describes a thought form which acquires a life of its own when it becomes the preserve of dark powers. On one level, people may bow down before a hand-carved block of wood or stone—something spiritually impotent, created in their own minds. On the other hand an evil spirit can infest the ritual object, thereby using the worshipper's adoration, fear or sacrificial offerings to its own advantage.

Death by name is far from impossible. In many cultures throughout history, incoming conquerors have practised a type of death by name. When James I of England allowed his aristocratic Scots followers to colonise Ireland through 'plantation' settlements, Irish families were not only forced out of their holdings but also compelled to change their names.

A change of name might not seem like such a big deal in the twenty-first century. Most westerners, when faced with the question of survival, would cheerfully give their name away if that's all it took. But names encode identity and destiny, so a forced change of name is an attempt to destroy the future for a family. Taking the land steals a physical inheritance but taking a name steals a spiritual one. The family loses their identity and, along with it, their destiny and calling.

One of Shing's ancestors was from the royal line of the Ming dynasty and was deeply respected, even by his enemies. When the Ming were overthrown and a rebel came to the throne, he was given an alternative to physical death: death by name change.

Although Shing only knew the story of the Shun emperor 'killing' her ancestor by stripping him of a royal name, it was possible to recognise how deeply the shame must have impacted him. Bitter and unforgiving, though no doubt secretly, he set in train a generational curse of death by name.

Centuries later, Shing's family was still using the practice. She was the unwanted girl, given an exalted male name to draw the attention of child-killing spirits.

Names are the fuse of life. They are the blessing God gives us to summon us into our calling, to remind us on a daily basis of who we are and what our destiny is. When they are used as a curse, then we have come into complicity with the satan and allowed him to steal another name and trade with it.

Such an alliance should be renounced in the company of witnesses, repented of and the grace of God requested to empower forgiveness from the heart for the perpetrators. Unspoken family beliefs such as, 'We're always robbed of our inheritance,' should be articulated, taken by faith to the Cross and renounced.

Shing's family lost everything of their rebuilt inheritance in Mao's Cultural Revolution. But it's not the physical building that counts—it's the spiritual inheritance.

On an ordinary, everyday level we can also practise death by name. We can bless people with a nickname meant to show affection or curse them with one meant to show contempt.

The same rules apply if we've been wounded by a nickname. If we hold resentment towards those who cursed our identity or if we refuse to forgive them, then we allow them to dictate who we are. We also allow them to kill our true identity and replace it with a false one. We come into agreement with the satan and give him the right to rob us of our calling and trade it in for a curse. We allow the slanderous nickname to find a resting place in our souls.

Again, such alliances with the Enemy should be renounced in the company of witnesses. We should repent of believing lies about ourselves and ask for the grace of God to forgive the perpetrators. Forgiveness is impossible unless God accomplishes it in us, so we need to ask for His empowerment. We may also need to request His grace to forgive ourselves for accepting the curse spoken over us. Any beliefs or vows about ourselves that came into being through a nickname should be articulated, taken by faith to the Cross and renounced.

Because it is at the Cross that we are made free.

Jesus took on all curses then, so that we—as His bride—might know fullness of life.

Destiny delayed is the devil's delight.

John Mason, You're Born an Original, Don't Die a Copy

The hint in Ezekiel 28 that the satan was trading names is reiterated elsewhere in Scripture. We are told in John 8:44 that the satan is a liar and the father of lies. Behind the Greek word, 'diabolos', is Hebrew 'kazab', *liar*, which has the basic sense of *building a false reputation of a name*. Slandering is just such a process of creating false reputation.

The Book of Job opens with the satan coming to the court of heaven and announcing he has been wandering to and fro in the earth. The word for *wandering to and fro* could also be translated *trading*. Perhaps the satan more accurately said, '*I've been on earth, trading,*' implying, '*I've been earthside, slandering.*'

Ezekiel however tells us he was walking between the fiery stones.

Two possibilities exist for the nature of the fiery stones—and ultimately these merge into one.

First, the fiery stones could be the living stones of the Church. We are fire and we are stones. Peter wrote:

'...you yourselves like living stones are being built up as a spiritual house, to be a holy priesthood to offer spiritual sacrifices acceptable to God through Jesus Christ. For it stands in Scripture:

"*Behold, I am laying in Zion a stone,*

> *a cornerstone chosen and precious,*
> *and whoever believes in Him will not be put to shame.'"*

1 Peter 2:5-6 ESV

These two verses contain a rich weaving of allusions to the threshold covenant rite and to Jesus as our cornerstone—He who is one with the flame-tongued Holy Spirit.

The Hebrew word for *being*, 'yesh', meaning *to exist* or *to have substance* has fire at its heart. Embedded in 'yesh' is 'esh' meaning *fire*. The very notion of having human substance is imbued with flame.

Rabbinic sages were said to have asked: 'Why is the word for *woman*, "ishah"?'

The answer: Because she is *fire*, 'esh'.

'Why is the word for *man*, "ish"?'

The answer: Because he too is *fire*, 'esh'.

We are souls of fire, we are living stones, we are walking names.

That's the first possibility for understanding the meaning of 'fiery stones'.

The second possibility lies behind the first and is only really distinguishable from it while we're thinking more like Greeks than Hebrews.

In Revelation 20, the satan is at last cast into the sea of fire where his allies have already been thrown. One of the most famous of all Hebrew scholars, Rabbi Solomon Yitzchaki, known as 'Rashi', lived almost a thousand years ago. He pointed out that heavens, 'shamayim', could mean *fire in waters*.[41]

True enough. The sea of fire—the sea of glass—could simply be *the heavens*.

Yet I think there's a far more obvious alternative than Rashi's: 'shamayim' could also be rendered as *sea of names*.[42]

Jewish philosophy is fructuous with the thought that Hebrew words and letters form the fabric of creation.[43] Poet Muriel Rukeyser expresses this concept in her famous line: 'The universe is made of stories, not of atoms.'

In the opening line of Genesis there's an untranslated word. It immediately precedes 'hashamayim', *the heavens*—the first created thing—and essentially tells us that words herald the act of creation, describe the method of creation, are the vessel of creation and the shape of it, as well as its witnesses.[44]

This untranslated word is comprised of alef and tav, the first and last letters of the Hebrew alphabet. The combination, like alpha to omega, symbolises the alphabet as a whole and, in addition, all possible combinations of them. Thus, every conceivable word.

Messianic believers see alef-tav as a reference to Jesus, the Word who was God and who was with God and who, pre-eminent above creation, existed before the foundation of the world.[45]

Now I won't suggest science agrees with this idea of words preceding creation but it certainly doesn't disagree. Current scientific theory suggests the universe came into being through sound. The question is: is that sound just random noise or is it encoded with meaning? And is there any real difference between a sound encoded with meaning and a word?

And, on a theological front, what's the difference between a word and a name? Names are relational: even small Indian orphans with serious mental impairment know that names are about belonging. They're about family.

Although I haven't been able to find any Jewish scholar who has translated 'hashamayim' as *the sea of names*, I find it fits well in many places.

The end of the satan and his cronies becomes a picture of poetic justice. The being without a name, who was probably expelled from the presence of God for trading names, is cast into the formless chaos of a sea of names and thereby forced to surrender all the names he has stolen.

And then comes a new heaven and a new earth.

The word of the Lord came to me:

'Son of man, say to the ruler of Tyre, "This is what the Sovereign Lord says: 'In the pride of your heart you say, "I am a god; I sit on the throne of a god in the heart of the seas." But you are a man and not a god...'"'

'Son of man, take up a lament concerning the king of Tyre and say to him: "This is what the Sovereign Lord says: 'You were the model of perfection, full of wisdom and perfect in beauty.

'You were in Eden, the garden of God; every precious stone adorned you: ruby, topaz and emerald, chrysolite, onyx and jasper, sapphire, turquoise and beryl. Your settings and mountings were made of gold; on the day you were created they were prepared.

'You were anointed as a guardian cherub, for so I ordained you. You were on the holy mount of God; you walked among the fiery stones.

'You were blameless in your ways from the day you were created till wickedness was found in you.

'Through your widespread trade you were filled with violence, and you sinned. So I drove you in disgrace from the mount of God, and I expelled you, O guardian cherub, from among the fiery stones...

'By your many sins and dishonest trade you have desecrated your sanctuaries...'"'

Ezekiel 28:1-2; 12-18 NIV

Quang was the fourth girl in her family. Her mother and father were under immense pressure before she was born—particularly from both grandmothers—to ensure the next child was a boy.

They consulted a fortune teller who advised them that the names of the three girls they already had did not form an auspicious pattern.

So they were all changed in an effort to create a situation which would be most favourable and conducive for the birth of a boy. The name changes didn't work: Quang arrived.

Despite the failure of all the changes to produce the desired result, none of her sisters reverted to their original names.

It's common in Asian cultures to use names as a form of manipulation and control: to summon a particular destiny for a child; to protect a child from harm, as in the case of Bruce Lee; to try to kill a child, as in Shing's case; or here, as for Quang, to achieve a desirable gender outcome.

Whenever a name is chosen, used or twisted in an effort to achieve a particular end, occult power is involved. The satan is getting what he wants: authority over a name so that its power can be used against itself. He's usurping an identity and a destiny—trading their glory in exchange for shame.

By getting his hooks into a name, he ensures that our family's inheritance is his. Our true birthright may well have been bargained away generations before we were born. And, where those bargains or occult contaminations involved covenantal vows, there is no time limitation on the agreement. There is nothing we can do to change a covenant: it lasts forever.

Fortunately while there's nothing we can do, there's plenty God can do. Through the death of Jesus, He has taken all curses for covenant-breaking onto Himself. Thus, when we come by faith before the cross of Jesus, we receive power to renounce any demonic covenants and to turn to God Himself.

When Your words came, I ate them; they were my joy and my heart's delight, for I bear Your name, Lord God Almighty.

Jeremiah 15:16 NIV

Throughout the gospels, Jesus generally shuns violence. He's constantly involved in conflict but He never lets the heat of the moment dictate His actions. He counsels His disciples to 'turn the other cheek', 'go the extra mile', 'love your enemies', 'do not return evil for evil.'

The notable exception to His peaceable, non-aggressive interaction with the world is the time He makes a whip out of cords and clears the Temple of the traders working in its precincts. Some scholars think there may have been two occasions this happened, since the story is recorded at the beginning of John's gospel and much later in Mark. However, as we have seen, John's gospel is crafted with incredible care to create a ring structure: unlike the recounting of the wedding feast at Cana or the first disciples following the Lamb John had just identified, there is no indication within the story itself that the Temple cleansing was early in Jesus' career. The placement in John's gospel may simply be to create a parallel with the empty tomb at the end.

Yet perhaps there's a deeper parallel. The satan was expelled from heaven for the abundance of his trade, his slander, his commodification of identity and destiny.

Why did Jesus target the money-changers who exchanged ordinary coinage into Temple shekels? Was it simply because this was a sacred precinct? At other times, after all, He paid taxes. And, on being asked a curly question about taxes, designed as entrapment, He asked for a coin and asked whose image it bore. When told it was Caesar, He offered the sage advice, 'Render to Caesar the things that are Caesar's and to God—the things that are God's.'

Caesar may have put his image on coins, but God puts His image on us. We are, according to Genesis 1:27, made male and female in the image of God. Jesus subtly reminded us to render our whole self to God.

But whose image was on the Temple shekels the money-changers were trading in the outer court? Caesar's? As stunning and unbelievable as it may seem, it was Melqart—a Phoenician god called 'Beelzebub', *lord of the flies*, by contemporary Israelites. The ancestors of these first century Jews would have known Melqart by another name still: Molech, the Canaanite god whose forbidden rites included the sacrifice of firstborn children in fire.

Melqart had been worshipped for over a millennium in centres like Tyre, Carthage and Cadiz.

Why on earth did the Temple priests permit such a sacrilege?

The Romans, in conquering Judea during the previous century, had forbidden the Jews to mint coins of their own. As a consequence, they had to buy them from elsewhere. Only shekels of the highest purity were considered worthy of use in the Temple and only the mint at Tyre provided such high quality silver. However this Tyrian shekel had a foreign god engraved on its front, an eagle on its back and included the words, 'Tyre, the Holy and Inviolable.'

Naturally, devout Jews did not carry these around: that would be to elevate Tyre to the level of the holy city, Jerusalem, as well as break the commandments prohibiting graven images and about having other gods before Yahweh.

Yet the Temple hierarchy had made a choice: rather than select an inferior class of metal, they decided to tolerate the proscribed image. They then forced their choice onto observant Jews, who were compelled to pay their Temple taxes by trading ordinary non-blasphemous coins for these supposedly superior shekels at exorbitant exchange rates.

Trade involving Tyre. The spiritual implications are immense.

No wonder Jesus was sick at heart. No wonder He was angry. No wonder He upturned the tables and lashed out with a whip.

Remember that He testified He did not do anything He did not see His Father in heaven doing. He expelled the traders from the Temple court just as the unnamed fallen cherub was expelled from the heavenly courts for trading. This same angelic entity—either the satan or the Angel of Death—was described prophetically centuries before in Ezekiel 28 as the spiritual power behind the Prince of Tyre. He had reasserted himself and begun trading again from Tyre. But he'd also set up headquarters in the heart of Jerusalem. In the outer court of the Temple precincts: what a beachhead.

If we look to John's parallel episode in his ring structure, we note that this incident corresponds to that of the empty tomb: the conquering of Death.

No doubt that is what we are really meant to see in this story about Jesus clearing the Temple: Death wants to put his stamp on our worship, wants us to trade with him as he slanders God, wants to take our identities and use their power to advance the kingdom of darkness, rather than light.

In many cases our ancestors made covenants with Death and, like the Jews in the first century, we're reaping the consequences of choices not our own. Covenants are normally forever—specifically excepting the covenant with Death which God says in Isaiah 28 He will annul.

Is it time to give Jesus permission to take out His whip? Only when we realise our own complicity with the spirits trading in various areas of our lives are we ready for His wild cleansing.

Your name is a golden bell hung in my heart. I would break my body to pieces to call you once by your name.

Peter S. Beagle, *The Last Unicorn*

The appearance of the Angel of Death in Scripture is often difficult to comprehend. No name. Just a title. One of the last enemies to be overcome.

Infamously present during the slaying of the firstborn, both men and cattle—the last of the ten plagues of Egypt, the one that finally convinced Pharaoh to let God's chosen people go.

Have we got this event the wrong way around, just as we've misunderstood the new birth?

Henry Clay Trumball suggested our concept of the Passover is inverted. The Israelites, in painting their doorposts with blood and allowing it to drip onto the cornerstone, were not sending a 'keep out' message to the Angel of Death. They were hanging a 'welcome' sign to invite God in.

Ancient, traditional rites of hospitality explain the event.[46] The *zebihat*, according to Abraham Mitrie Rihbany in *The Syrian Christ*, was still performed in the twentieth century. Rihbany connects *zebihat* to the visit of God to Abraham at Hebron while Trumball connects it to the Passover.

If a householder knew a visitor was coming, he'd kill a calf or goat on the threshold of the home. He'd then paint the blood on the doorposts and lintel so that, as the guest approached, he would know a feast was prepared in his honour. He would be assured of a welcome by the host. A kiss of greeting. Washing and anointing for his feet. His visit treated as an occasion for celebration and joy. Most importantly of all, according to Trumball, a covenant undertaken.

If a guest chose to *pass over* the blood on the threshold, as opposed to *trampling* or *stumbling* and defiling it, he was indicating his willingness to covenant with the householder. The host and the guest were then obliged to defend each other to the death. The vows of a covenant effectively say: 'I will do anything to protect you. I will tear myself apart before I go back on this promise.' This is why Lot offers his daughters to the men of Sodom, rather than give up the men under his care. A covenant was involved.

According to Trumball, at the first Passover the signs of hospitality were out to welcome God in as covenant defender. At this time, men still retained their position as priest in their own family and thus each fulfilled a priestly role in sacrificing the lamb.

God therefore, in accepting the invitation and passing over the threshold, came into relationship with the family as their covenant defender, their divine protector. He would have actually been their guardian, shielding them against all comers, including the Angel of Death.

Once we accept the threshold covenant changes the nature of what's happening at the Passover, we have to also look carefully at the role of the Angel of Death. Who sent him to kill the firstborn of Egypt? Why were the cattle involved? Why didn't the Angel of Death enter houses marked with the blood of a lamb?

Generally speaking texts like Exodus 12:23 are translated to say God passed through and struck the Egyptians. Yet 'nagaph' the word for *smite* or *strike* is also the word for *stumble*. It is translated *dash* in Psalm 91:12 NKJV: *In their [the angels'] hands they shall bear you up, lest you dash your foot against a stone.*

The word for *passing through*, 'abar, can also mean *pass over*. It is used in speaking of a blood covenant to refer to the part of the ceremony known as 'the walk of blood'. It may also be a pun on the names Hebron, Hebrew and Abraham: Hebron meaning *a passage* and the location of three of God's four covenants with Abraham, the first man to be called an Ebru—or Hebrew.[47]

Its wordplay would therefore indicate the God who is passing over is indeed the covenant-keeping ever-living One of Abraham, Isaac and Jacob.

Moreover, *passing over* and *stumbling* are actions specifically used in reference to a threshold stone. They are key words indicating the guest's attitude towards the invitation and they specify whether the visitor is willing to cut covenant with the host.

All this points to another possible rendering of Exodus 12:23— 'When the Lord goes through the land to strike down the Egyptians, He will see the blood on the top and sides of the doorframe and will *pass over* that doorway, and He will not permit the destroyer to enter your houses and strike you down.'

Could it therefore be this is meant to read that God will pass over, while Egypt stumbles? That He will pass over the threshold stone and prevent the destroyer from trampling on it?

If the implication of the Egyptians stumbling is that they had trampled on the threshold stone, then they had no covenant defender. When the Angel of Death arrived, they were perilously vulnerable.

Who sent this fallen cherub to kill the firstborn of both humans and cattle? In a very real sense, the Egyptians themselves did.

One of Scripture's most prominent laws is: *you reap what you sow*. When you bless others, blessing will return to you. When you perpetuate evil, you'll eventually be overtaken by it. Justice might be slow in coming—it might not appear for decades—but, sooner or later, it has its day.

The Book of Exodus opens with the mass killing of infants—all boys. In many cases, firstborn sons. Pharaoh issued commands to some midwives to eliminate all newborn Israelite males. When the midwives shirk this duty, Pharaoh then orders his people to throw the baby boys into the river Nile.

Because these were Pharaoh's orders, then everything under his authority—all Egypt, including land, animals and people—would reap the consequences. These natural consequences of spiritual law would inevitably involve drowning and other fatalities for his children or their children as well as the mass of Egyptians.

More than eighty years passed before the consequences rolled around. The Angel of Death, a cherub like the satan, came to Egypt because he had the legal right to do so. Pharaoh had sowed death and, in doing so, had invited Death on a state visit.

The problem was that Death is an opportunist as well as a legalist. On the one hand, he might have restricted himself to just retribution, but on the other hand, the Israelites were still under Pharaoh's rule. They were fair game. Had God not become the covenant defender of the Hebrews then, in every house, they would clearly have lost their firstborn sons too.

Many of us, unknowingly, have covenants with Death, rather than God. Our ancestors took them out and we have never repudiated them.

5

The Sea of Names

NEARLY FOUR THOUSAND YEARS ago, a twinkle of light left a faint pulsating star in the southern constellation Serpens. Orbiting that particular pulsar, J1719-1438, are the leftovers of a massive star which has been reduced to crystalline carbon. A diamond is crystalline carbon, so this is a stunning oversized gem in the sky.

Four thousand years is around the time Abram first covenanted with God. Looking up at the jewelled pavement of heaven we call the Milky Way, Abram was told his descendants would be as uncountable as the stars. At the very moment he became a 'Friend of God', a sparklet of starlight from that diamond-circled sun in Serpens began its long journey across the galaxy heading for earth. It's about to arrive.

When it was halfway here, a mote of light from a different quarter of space—a star in the Great Nebula of Orion—set off towards us. About the time Jesus was sitting in the Temple as a twelve-year-old boy, confounding the scholars of His generation, that gleam hurtled off on its way to this small ocean-blue planet. It too is about to arrive.

When it does, it will join with starlight from the walls of heaven—from the very edge of the visible universe. That light has been travelling so long it comes from the beginning of the cosmos.

This starlight from the walls of heaven will join with light that left its sun just as the first block in the Great Wall of China was laid. They will mix with other light that set off as Babylonian armies breached the walls of Jerusalem, and with still other that started just as the Roman armies razed those rebuilt walls half a millennium later.

Let's get technical. All of these tiny packets of light—called photons—travel towards us at the same phenomenally fast rate. The 'speed of light' is roughly seven times around the earth each second.

Suppose we can interrogate these photons as they arrive. We'll start with a photon from J1719-1438: 'How long did it take you to get here?'

'No time at all,' it will answer. 'I just left. Not even a second ago.'

Huh? Not four thousand years? Baffled, we might turn to a photon from the Orion Nebula. 'How long did it take *you* to get here?'

'No time at all,' it will answer. 'I just left. Not even a second ago.'

But shouldn't the answer be two millennia? More puzzled, we might turn to some photons just in from the walls of heaven. *Aha, we might think. A chance to solve that vexing question about the age of the universe. An opportunity to find out once and for all who's right: the young earth creationists or the scientific theorists who advocate billions of years.*[48]

The photons look incredibly jaunty for motes of light as old as the cosmos itself. They don't look ruinously ancient or remotely decrepit. 'How long did it take you guys to get here?' we ask.

'No time at all,' they'll answer. 'We just left. Not even a second ago.'

As far as these photons are concerned, the beginning of the universe is *now*.

As far as the photons of J1719-1438 are concerned, there's no time lapse of four thousand years between the era of Abram and the present day. As for the photons of the Orion Nebula, the first and twenty-first centuries are contiguous.[49]

Mind-bending.

Time isn't static. The theory of relativity discovered by Albert Einstein reveals that it depends on how fast we travel.

We don't normally notice time discrepancies because we don't have any transportation capable of getting us from one hemisphere to another in a second or less.

But if that were possible,[50] we'd notice time becoming seriously warped. If we could hitch a lift in a vehicle travelling at the speed of light, no time would pass for us while it would tick along the same as ever for anyone watching us.[51]

The movie *Interstellar* showcases the wide distortion in experiential time due to relativistic effects. When Cooper and Brand return from a few hours of atmospheric insertion on an oceanic planet, they discover 23 years have passed on the waiting space station. What for them has been raw minutes of heart-stopping, adrenaline-injected, near-catastrophic adversity has been slow decades of routine maintenance and long-collapsed hope for the lone astronaut left behind.

Time and eternity are tightly entangled. It's no coincidence, in my view, that much of our basic scientific language about light is related to the sea—currents, waves, streams. Just as the Jewish word for *day* is derived from the word for *sea*. In every other language I've investigated it's conceptually related to sunlight. However in Hebrew thought it's related to 'the deep'.

JRR Tolkien in *The Silmarillion* developed a creation story featuring a vast and splendid angelic song which perceptively used the phrase 'the deeps of time'.

Perhaps it's no coincidence that space was once referred to as 'the deeps', just as the sea was. Or that 'astronaut' means *star sailor*, from 'aster', *star*, and nautical, *sea-related*.

The space-time continuum is an astoundingly complex place.

Four thousand years ago[52] God asked Job, *'Where were you when I laid the foundations of the earth? ...who laid its cornerstone when all the morning stars sang together and the sons of God shouted for joy?'*

The mystery of relativity means we can actually participate in that praise-filled celebration. *As it happens.*

Light from the morning stars still reaches earth each moment. Unobtrusively, as part of the background, their majestic song is happening right now. Tonight, we could gaze up at the grandeur of the heavens, experience starlight from the beginning of time and combine our voices with their cries of wonder. Wouldn't it be absolutely awesome to take part in the first song of creation?

There's a beautiful scene in CS Lewis' classic children's fantasy, *The Chronicles of Narnia*, where Digory and Polly witness the birth of the world of Narnia, accompanied by star-song. The breath of the Lion awakens all Narnia into thinking, speaking and loving; everything—its animals, its trees, its waters. The story should remind us of a line from another song:

The heavens were made by the Word of the Lord and all the stars by the breath of His mouth.

Psalm 33:6 GWT

It doesn't take much for us to experience a mystery as marvellous and awe-inspiring as the creation of Narnia. The great wonder of Einstein's theory of relativity is this: all it takes to witness the song of the morning stars as the heavens and the earth were created is to walk outside and look up.

When we can experience a change of meaning—a new meaning—there we may rightly join hands and sing with the morning stars; for there we are in at the birth. There is one of the exact points at which the genius, the originality, *of the individual writer has first entered the world.*

Owen Barfield, *Poetic Diction: A Study in Meaning*

Did you?

Did you pause at the end of the last section and go outside and raise your voice in song? Did you take the opportunity to join intentionally with the angels—the sons of God—and the morning stars? I hope you did. I hope you decided to let your voice melt into the first choir of all time and participate in the soul-piercing wonder of its never-ceasing praise.

If you haven't done so yet, wait. There's another matter I'd love you to consider.

We've been supposing that we could interview photons as they arrived. Let's go further and suppose these photons could turn the tables on us. Probably their first question would be: 'What is the news from heaven?'

Now remember: the last thing they know about is the creation of a stunningly beautiful and immaculate universe.

What headline succinctly encapsulates the events of all time since? My vote is for this: 'The Son of God has been raised from the dead.'

That statement isn't a simple one. It's a wondrous proclamation, carrying an almost unbearable weight of implication: the birth, the death, the resurrection of Jesus. The existence of death, corruption entering a perfect world, a divine plan to restore justice and peace without ignoring righteousness and truth, long ages when the Judge of all the earth holds back on pronouncing a final sentence, remaining compassionate and faithful while mankind reaps the consequences of not turning back to Him.

We could go on and on with more and more detail. We could mention the Bride of the Son of God and how she arrived through a pierced side.

The photons would probably nod at that. 'Aha! We were there at the first birthing and the prophetic piercing.' Whatever else surprised them, the piercing of the Word wouldn't.

And, if we told such a story, we'd be performing an angelic task, even though most of us would feel pretty silly talking to starlight.

Jesus Himself gave us a mandate to do an angelic task, to be His messengers, His ambassadors. He told us to take the good news of salvation to the whole of creation. Francis of Assisi took this very seriously; he preached to the birds and animals as well as the Sultan of Damietta, a nephew of Saladin.

'We are starstuff.' With these words, the eminent cosmologist, Carl Sagan, poetically expressed his belief that we have been fathered by eons-long galactic processes along with random atomic and chemical reactions.

Francis of Assisi would disagree. In his stirring hymn, *Brother Sun, Sister Moon*, he wrote of both the animate and inanimate creation as our siblings. We are not descended from the stars: they, like us, have both been created by the same loving Father. GK Chesterton points out that this insight of Francis came at the perfect historical moment: if it had come any earlier—when the average person still saw a god in the sun, a goddess in the moon, nymphs in trees and rivers, fauns and satyrs guarding flocks and herds—then a new syncretistic religion would have arisen.

This insight is an important message, not just for the medieval era in which Francis lived, but for our own era. In the polarised debates over climate change, there are two extremes:

- those who honour the earth so much their worship verges on idolatry
- those who abuse it so much their despoliation is almost a straight line back to the kind of trading that was the satan's speciality

Amongst the slander and propaganda, it's almost impossible for the average Christian who deeply desires to steward the earth to sift out any truth.

'Thou canst not stir a flower without troubling of a star,' said Francis Thompson, reflecting the ancient belief all creation is linked together and our actions on earth have heavenly consequences. Today we might, slightly more scientifically, reframe his words into the concept of the Butterfly Effect: the discovery that infinitesimally small changes in initial weather conditions have enormously different long-term consequences. Edward Lorenz, the discoverer of this phenomenon, likened the situation to a hurricane which can trace its origin back to the flapping of a butterfly's wings several weeks earlier.

This clay ball of earth with its core of iron is looking forward to its redemption as much as we should be. Like the rest of creation, it is waiting to be released from futility and in the meantime strains '*on tiptoe to see the wonderful sight of the sons of God coming into their own.*' (Romans 8:19 JB Phillips)

Our concern for the redemptive healing of the earth should parallel our concern for the redemptive healing of all humanity.

Mathematics is the art of giving the same name to different things.[53]

Jules Henri Poincaré

I love impact craters. Sure, a lot of people scratch their heads about my enthusiasm for what they see as very unremarkable holes in the ground, but that only goes to show how easy it is to overlook beauty that doesn't conform to the ordinary.

My interest began on reading a feature article in an astronomy magazine in which Eugene Shoemaker waxed lyrical about the astrobleme, *star scar*, at Gosse Bluff in Central Australia. Speaking of the shattercones found there, he said that the waveprints in them were a message preserved in rock from the moment of impact.

'What,' I wondered, 'would God have to say that's so important that He had to slam a comet into the earth to write a message in the rock?'

Only a few years earlier, I had stayed up very late to watch the live broadcast of the first Mars landing. As the Viking lander sent back the first pictures of a desolate landscape, I remember my first, instinctive reaction: 'This place has been destroyed. An entire planet. Why did You do that, God?'

Perhaps the question about Mars is unanswerable but I

was always sure that, with just a little bit of help from the Holy Spirit, it would be possible to decipher the message written in the shattercones of Gosse Bluff.

So I went there. I bought a massive shattercone—sometimes more romantically called 'angel wings', 'angel hair' or 'mare's tails'—from the Ries crater in Germany just so I'd know exactly what I was looking for. I photographed the shattercones at Gosse Bluff and soon realised that, as I'd suspected, it wasn't all that hard to read the message in the rock. It was simply a matter of translating the mathematics of a special geometric form into everyday English.

And, bowl me over, if another realisation didn't immediately hit me. It wasn't necessary to go to Central Australia to find that message from God. I could simply have walked out into my garden, picked any flower, and found the same geometry. In fact, I didn't need to go as far as my garden. I could have looked at my hands or my face and found the same basic mathematics there.

Within the deeps of time something remarkable is visible to the mathematician: the universe in dominated by innumerable variations on one single design, commonly called the 'golden ratio' or 'divine proportion'. Is there anywhere you can go in the universe, anything natural you can look at or listen to that *doesn't* contain the mathematics of the golden ratio somewhere in its structure? I'm really confident there isn't. I've tried—very hard at times—to find something that *doesn't* contain the mathematics of the golden ratio. And I've failed. Every time I've thought I've found something that *doesn't* have it, a closer analysis revealed that it did.

So it seems to me that everything does. Everything.

Not exactly. Not perfectly. But, in the vast majority of cases, far too closely for coincidence.

The great wheeling spirals of galactic arms, the pulses emanating from the Crab Nebula, the division in the rings of Saturn, the wild spinning winds of a whirlwind seen from space, the inferior conjunctions of Venus.

The intersecting seed spirals on the head of a sunflower, on the bracts of a pineapple or the scales of a pinecone, on a fuzzy-headed dandelion or a red clover flower, on a purple-bearded thistle or verdant green broccoli or the delicate flowerets of Queen Anne's Lace.

In the coiled tail of a seahorse or a chameleon, in the unfolding fiddlehead of a young fern, in the cross-section of a nautilus shell or a fossil ammonite, the feathers of a lyrebird, the barbels on a peacock's tail, the pearlescent architectural shape inside an abalone, the mouflons of a ram, the curve of an elephants' tusk, a dolphin's fin, a bird's beak, a zebra's stripes, the bandings of a fish, the markings on a butterfly's wings, the interleaving of leaves on celery or leeks, the arrangement of the envelope of petals on a rose.

In the shape of a starfish or the markings on a sand dollar. In the turret and turban and trumpet shapes of thousands of different kinds of seashells. In the pentagram found by cutting across a pear, an apple or a papaya. In the five-petal arrangement of a dog rose, blue borage, frangipani or hundreds of other flowers.

Why are bananas bent? Because, like the shattercones at Gosse Bluff with their segments of logarithmic spirals, they contain a message from God.

That message is also written across and within the human body: in the whorl of hair at the crown of a head, the size of one tooth compared to its neighbour, the beat of a heart, the most comfortable body temperature, the coil of the Eustachian tubes inside the ear, the comparative sizes of bones in the fingers, the dimensions of a chromosome. It's to be found in the dimensions of the orbitals within a hydrogen atom, as well as in the transition from Newtonian mechanics to Einstein's relativity.

Wherever you look, the golden ratio is there. It's inescapable. As we look around the universe with open and alert eyes, we would be able to record millions upon millions of design variations, using the golden ratio as the starting point. The Greeks considered it to be an ideal of beauty and so, because many governments have copied their architecture, multitudes of buildings—both ancient and modern—have incorporated it as part of the design. The Greeks called it: 'the logos'.

That name may give us a hint as to why it can be found absolutely everywhere. *In the beginning*, wrote John the apostle, *was the Word*—the 'logos'. But 'logos' doesn't just mean *word*—it also means *reason*, *ratio*, *mind* and *wisdom*. It had a mathematical connotation, a rational, logical[54] one and a verbal one. Moreover, when used in a mathematical sense, '*the*' ratio to the Greeks meant the golden ratio.

All of this means it should come as no surprise to find the golden ratio hidden in the gematria underlying Genesis 1:1 as well as several more times in the mathematical structure of the opening chapter.[55] It is the creation blueprint. It's therefore logical to find the mathematical 'logos' hidden in the design of the creation account.

But what does it say? Is it possible to decipher the epistle written in the waveprints of the rocks of Gosse Bluff?

Now I can't take credit for this translation. Centuries before I was born, mathematicians like Luca Pacioli—friend and mentor to Leonardo da Vinci—and Jakob Bernoulli had already written about it. Medieval poets structured their writing in ways that ensured key words or structural breaks appeared right at the golden ratio position. By analysing the commonalities of their works, it's possible to discern what they understood by the 'logos'.

As I have indicated in much fuller detail along with some mathematical analysis in *The Singing Silence*, the message of the golden ratio is: *God is trinity, God is love, God is resurrection and life.*

Although it's blazoned across the universe, neither Pacioli nor Bernoulli, nor any medieval poet nor an ancient Greek architect, can be credited with discovering its existence. That honour, it would appear, goes to the magi—the astronomers, astrologers, mathematicians and diviners—of ancient Babylon. They uncovered it around the mid-sixth century BC, during the period when they were led by the prophet Daniel.

Soon after this time, quadratic concepts were brought to the west by Pythagoras, who studied with the magi after being captured in

Egypt by the armies of Cambyses and carted off to Babylon. Pythagoras was allegedly so entranced by the golden ratio that later biographies suggest he made the pentagram—the five-pointed star which infinitely encodes it—the symbol of his Brotherhood.

Yet, as I point out in *The Singing Silence*, Daniel is far more likely to be its discoverer. We have the testimony of Daniel in the book bearing his own name but our knowledge of Pythagoras largely dates from stories written down eight hundred years after his death. Daniel not only mentions a lot of mysterious numbers—mysterious not in the sense the numbers are enigmatic but how and when they should be applied certainly is—he also recorded a visit by an angelic 'palmoni'—*a revealer of the secrets of numbers*—and, while there's no evidence the angel told him about quadratic formulation, it's all too easy to use a five-pointed star as a prophecy pointing to the return of a Jewish king. The Jewish people believed that God wrote words in the stars—it wasn't a long stretch for them to consider He'd leave a message even within a drawing of a star.

Especially, if they happened to note—as I'm sure Daniel would have—that the golden ratio is to be found within the gematria of the very first line of the Pentateuch, Genesis 1:1.

Now, besides the information stored within the pentagram itself, only one extra piece of information is needed to know exactly where and when the Messiah would be born: a starting point for the time calculation. And if you were to use the fall of Babylon and the whisking away of the prophet Daniel to Persia as this starting point, you might well—when it got close to 540 years later—persuade a group of magi to make the trip west for this long-foretold historic event.

Just where would the mathematics of a five-pointed star lead you? Well, if you continued to follow the exact latitude encoded in the star, you would eventually have to pass through a little Judean village called Bethlehem.

It's the most logical answer in the entire cosmos, yet it is still so surprising.

Whether the magi at the time of Jesus followed an abstract mathematical diagram or a star in the heavens—be it comet, conjunction of planets or supernova—it doesn't really make any difference. Everything, absolutely everything, in the entire universe points to the line of latitude that passes through Bethlehem!

As a potter signs his work, so God as a Master Potter has stamped all His creation with a strong, consistent signature. It's a wondrous mathematical autograph that, no matter what human language you speak, gives the same message in translation: *I am trinity, I am love, I am resurrection and life.*

Oh, and find Me at Bethlehem.

In the beginning...

Genesis 1:1
John 1:1

In the beginning was the Word—the Ratio, the Reason, the Wisdom—*and the Word*—the Ratio, the Reason, the Wisdom—*was with God and the Word*—the Ratio, the Reason, the Wisdom—*was God.*

I've often wondered how different western civilisation would be if, centuries ago, the translators of Scripture had chosen to render 'logos' as *ratio*. For a start, mathematics would be far more highly valued in general society; not simply as a tool but as a creative artform rivalling any inspired aspect of literature. People wouldn't look at me strangely for examining the mathematical aspects of Scripture, wondering if I'm dabbling in some arcane mystery. They wouldn't buy into the idea that the 'scribes' at the time of Jesus were primarily writers and copyists—when their title, in fact, means *the ones who count*. Even experts wouldn't disdain Jerome's Vulgate so much if it were more widely realised that Jerome was attempting, as David Howlett has demonstrated, to translate from Hebrew into Latin, while preserving *both* the literary sense and the mathematical structure.

To confine creativity to art, craft, music and literature and never realise it's possible to revel in creative mathematics like John's or Paul's, as they were inspired by the Holy Spirit into some amazing arithmetical design, is a sad indictment on the way we think.

Translation of Scripture is such a responsible task we will be judged accordingly for it.

In the beginning, God created...

Instinctively we fill in the void with: *the heavens and the earth.*

Beautiful as this is, I wonder if we're really sounding the deeps with this particular translation.

Rashi, you may recall, translated 'hashamayim', *the heavens*, as *fire in waters* or the *sea of fire*.

And I've suggested it could be rendered as *the sea of names*.

This begs an obvious question. If 'shamayim' is *sea of names*, what is 'erets', usually translated *earth*?

When I first considered the possibility of *sea of names* and discovered the only obvious alternative interpretation of 'erets' was to do with *breaching, breaking out* or *piercing*,[56] I hesitated. I was baffled for months.

It never occurred to me initially to consider *piercing* in the light of spiritual birth, the spear in the side of Christ or the creation of Eve. Re-imaging *earth* as a *piercing* was confusing: my heart was inclined to believe it was right but, to my head, it was a nonsense riddle.

A piercing in what? Space? But what is space? Or what, for that matter, is matter? What we think of as a chair solid enough to sit on is, in fact, not a dense conglomeration of atoms but almost entirely empty. A cloud of quantum possibilities. A fold in fieldlines, a knot of electromagnetism and gravity and other fundamental forces.

'Piercing' was mind-warping, even within the boggling context of modern physics.

Yet it taunted me—it niggled at my sense the heavens as the sea of names had much to recommend it as an idea. It also eroded my confidence that it could be a legitimate alternative, even if *piercing* wasn't.

Then it all clicked into place while I was listening to Ian Johnson speak on the wounds of Christ as our entry into His Body, and the parallel between the creation of Eve and the birth in water and spirit of the Church. The church: those whose names were written in the Book of Life belonging to the *'Lamb slain from the foundation of the world.'* (Revelation 13:8 NKJV) The Lamb who was pierced by spear and thorn but whose bones were not broken.

To think this spiritual rebirth was prophesied deep within the opening line of Genesis: as early as the seventh word!

Genesis 1:1, as I have indicated in *God's Panoply*, is a masterpiece of mathematics and poetry. It apparently encodes a stunningly accurate value for π. But its mathematics also encodes the numbers associated with covenant, 111 and 1111. Ivan Panin points out that the numerical value of the words *God*, *heaven* and *earth* total 777 which goes beyond covenant into suggesting God kissed His creation into being.[57] Further, this opening line says in the plainest possible mathematical language that God is trinity, is love, is resurrection and life.

A fusion of mathematics and poetry describing the time before the foundation of the world? Science would be delighted with the first and horrified with the second. Yet I'm reminded of the thought of Dylan Thomas: 'A good poem helps to change the shape and significance of the universe, helps to extend everyone's knowledge of himself and the world around him.'[58]

The cosmos being sculpted by poetry? Verse singing the universe into shape?

This insight called to mind a medieval poem alluding to the integration of Five Wounds on the Cross within the shield of faith, to the kiss of heaven and earth and the sustaining song of the angel host. I was reminded, yet again, of the profound depths of Hebraic thinking in the works of the author of *Sir Gawain and the Green Knight*.[59] Those despised medievals, I sighed to myself, knew a thing or two we've forgotten.

The poetic hymns that open Genesis and John's gospel are not as obviously songs as those, for example, in the Finnish mythic cycle, *Kalevala*, where the godling Väinämöinen works creation magic through the bardic songs he sings. Nor are they as obvious as the wondrous song Aslan sings in *The Magician's Nephew* to birth the world of Narnia.

Mostly because they're not labelled that way. And because poetry is, of course, the first casualty of translation.

Even so I wondered: is Genesis 1 really poetry? Is it the kind of verse that could sing the universe into shape?

On an old crumpled piece of paper torn out of a notebook I once used at a seminar are these lines from an unidentified speaker: 'Poetry is unsung music. Poetry is what sings the universe into shape.'

It's a very, very old idea, not a new one. Poetry connects to the heart and emotions, trying to convey a truth and evoke a response. To relate.

But there's a stunning mathematical sub-structure too, appealing to the mind. Seeking to provoke wonder, awe, worship.

Yet, if we concede this point about poetry, would it nevertheless be more accurate to say that *naming* sings the universe into shape? That the name of God is the ignition spark?

The first word God is recorded as speaking in the command, 'Let there be light!' is *be*, יהי from היה. And this is the sacred name given to Moses at the burning bush: Ehyeh.

Names embody identity and destiny. Why not embody the entire universe?

Living so that you beautify your name, even if it wasn't beautiful to begin with... making it stand in people's thoughts for something so lovely and pleasant that they never think of it by itself.

Lucy Maud Montgomery, *Anne of Avonlea*

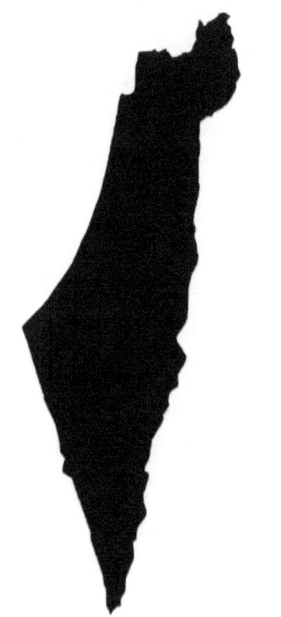

A modern outline map of Ha'aretz Israel—the land of Israel—reveals an extraordinary secret.

Ha'aretz, *the land*, derives from erets, *earth*, relating—in my view—to 'ratsa", *pierce*.

Note the shape of the country: like a piercing tool.

God continues to keep faithful watch over the words He used to bring the cosmos into being.

As the Master Potter, those words include every name He's ever breathed into clay to create souls like yours and mine.

There is no music in a 'rest' but there's the making of music in it. And people are always missing that part of the life melody.

John Ruskin

Hallowed *be* Your name.

When Jesus taught His disciples to pray at their request, He started with *Father* and *heaven* and *name*. A natural combination since before the beginning of time.

The very first name covenant was not that between God and Abraham.

It was between God and all creation.

The reason six days elapse between
- the name and threshold covenants God cut with Abraham
- the name and threshold covenants Jesus cut with Peter
- the name covenant Jesus cut with Mary Magdalene, and the Passover
- Yom Kippur, *the Day of Atonement*, and Sukkot, *the Feast of Booths*
- in a natural parallel, the fertilisation of a woman's egg and its implantation[60] in the womb

is simply because they reflect the original cosmic covenants. The first name covenant occurred at the creation of the sea of names. It may not be obvious in the wording but there's more than just words in the verse. Covenant, as I've indicated in *God's Panoply*,[61] is built into the mathematical sub-structure of the opening line—along with the golden ratio which tells us so much about the nature of God. The original name covenant occurred on the first day of creation and the original threshold covenant on the sixth: when God created the image-bearer and regent to whom He would gift the art of naming. In naming the animals, Adam spoke over the seed of the word, already fertilised by God, and implanted it into the womb of the world. Creation 'took', so to speak.

We can also see through this that a threshold covenant is a precursor to entering into rest.

As we enter our destiny, we enter into the Sabbath of God.

These cosmic covenants were violated at the time Adam fell.

'Where are you (hidden)?' the Lord God asked him, while he and Eve concealed themselves in the Garden after eating the fruit.

Such a simple question. Yet it is fraught with such deep implication: it indicates dissolution of oneness and a fragmentation into one plus one.

It reveals the covenant was broken.

Long ages later, Mary Magdalene in another garden asks an almost reciprocal question: 'Where is my Lord hidden?' She was participating in her own threshold covenant—a time of coming into the destiny inscribed[62] in her name.

All godly thresholds, physical or spiritual, require by God's command a memorial to His salvation acts. Observant Jews place a mezuzah on a doorpost in obedience to God's direction in Deuteronomy 6:9 to remember Him every time they go out and in. It is considered a watch over the door, a symbolic 'keeper of memory'.

The name Magdalene, meaning *from Magdala*, preserves this sense of *memorial watchtower*. Mary Magdalene's destiny was to be the keeper of memory when it came to the most significant event of all the ages: the resurrection of the Messiah. I'm sure that every time Peter or John got one of the minor details wrong about what happened that morning, she made sure they corrected their inaccuracy in the next retelling.

The resurrection was a time of covenant restoration—when the reversal of curses became possible.

There's often a tendency to say, 'It's all done at the Cross,' and to understand this statement as meaning every kind of sin is automatically dealt with, eliminating any need for further action on the part of a believer. This includes generational iniquity, curses following family lines and national upheaval. This theology however fails to recognise the significance of Jesus' own actions: the story of Thomas and his doubts is about the lifting of a curse that had afflicted every Israelite since the time Moses sent twelve spies to scout out the Promised Land about 1500 years previously. The curse wasn't automatically nullified just because Jesus had died on the Cross.[63]

In John's structural chiasmus, the story of 'doubting' Thomas at the gospel's end mirrors the story at the beginning about Nathanael and his doubts. Curiously, this is the only time in the whole ring design the names aren't paired exactly. The usual coupling is Mary with Mary, Nicodemus with Nicodemus, John with John, Peter and the other disciples with Peter and the other disciples.

Yet, a closer look reveals that perhaps Nathanael and Thomas are more subtly paired. Nathanael is only mentioned twice in Scripture: both times in John's gospel. Because his name does not appear in any other list of disciples, it's long been considered he is the same disciple as Bartholomew, meaning *son of Ptolemy*.

Immediately this brings us to the right name link. Both Thomas and Ptolemy are likely to be derived from the same root, 'telem', *to furrow* and to be related to another name, Talmai. This unusual name appears just a few times in Scripture.

The king of Geshur who was the father-in-law of king David and also the grandfather of Absalom was named Talmai. So was one of the giants the twelve spies encountered on first entering the Promised Land. Perhaps that's not a coincidence: obviously something very odd was present in Absalom's genetic makeup to enable him to grow such mountains of hair at such a prodigious rate (2 Samuel 14:26).

Talmai and his brothers caused ten of twelve spies to have doubts.

Ten of twelve disciples had no doubts while Thomas (and Judas) did.

The situations are reversed when Jesus brings to death all that is left from this ancient curse.

Sometimes our lives are like this. The remnants of 'stuff' that occurred hundreds of years ago still affect us. Because of name covenants taken out at the very inception of our family line or because of threshold covenant violation somewhere along the centuries, we are reaping consequences that have nothing to do with our individual actions but everything to do with us as corporate beings in a family.

Instead of cherubim guarding the threshold into our destinies, dark spiritual rulers—like Python, Rachab and Leviathan—may be present instead.

And instead of entering into rest, we may find instead a fouled mare's nest. Here I am using the term, 'mare's nest', in its archaic sense—that of an entangled spiritual mess where the spirits of nightmare have taken up residence. The nest may be made up of broken dreams, good intentions never followed through, half-kept promises, hidden motives, unfulfilled hopes, false forgiveness—excusing and tolerating, rather than judging and pardoning.

These spiritual spoilers have made a nest, right where we have been promised rest.

And we need a whirlwind of grace from the Holy Spirit to blow them all away. So that our name and threshold covenants with Jesus are not infested, contaminated or defiled but, instead in every way, proclaim: 'Hallowed be *Your* name.'

6

Sentinels on the Threshold

WHAT IS GRACE?

Somehow we've come to see it as opposed to law, when in fact, as I have argued in *God's Panoply*, law is an aspect of God's grace. In a society without law, the whim of the biggest, meanest, strongest and wealthiest is the rule.

Although we should know better, grace is understood by many Christians to mean that we don't have to obey the law anymore—that we are free of legalistic constraint and can decide for ourselves how to behave. In theory, the Holy Spirit is our guide and conscience; in practice, all too often our own desires are. Far too many people leave the local church—if not forever, then often for a decade or more—because of wounds inflicted and injustices perpetrated by Christians in their own community. Christians who see themselves as forgiven as a result of God's grace while perceiving their wounded brother or sister as the real offender because they struggle to forgive, rather than offering pardon freely and instantly.

Freedom from rigid, legalistic bonds doesn't confer on us a licence for immorality. We know that. But in our carnal desire to excuse our own shortcomings, we look at Paul's writings on grace, divorcing them from what Jesus said, rather than examining them in that light.

Instead of a glorious uplifting and ennobling, grace has become perverted into an excuse for accepting sin—the very thing Paul warned about. We use it to maintain our self-esteem, instead of grieving the wounds we've inflicted on others. We trample on the sacrifice of the

Cross, just as an invited guest would despise the host's invitation by trampling on the threshold stone. Such an attitude towards grace shows contempt for God's covenant.

One of the foremost reasons for older Christians dropping their church attendance and developing 'private' religion is their treatment by others in Christ's Body. It shouldn't be so.

The Ten Commandments were, and are, radical and uncompromising.

Many scholars will point out that similar law systems, such as the Code of Hammurabi, existed at the time Moses delivered the Commandments at Mount Sinai. But that, as Rabbi Joel Hoffman has indicated, is to miss their revolutionary nature.[64] Don't kill. Don't steal. Don't commit adultery.

Just don't.

Because they're wrong.

The Law of Moses is about morality; the other codes are about fear of penalty.

Paul describes himself in Philippians 3:6 NIV this way: '*...as for righteousness based on the Law, faultless...*'

It might seem, at that moment, he was self-aggrandising and somewhat delusional. But the reality is that many people go through life without killing or committing adultery; some people even manage to go through life without stealing.

The new atheists insist it's possible to be 'good without God'—basing their claim on the fact many non-believers outdo Christians in acts of generosity, kindness and even self-sacrifice. In addition, many are scrupulously honest, faithful to their spouse and have never murdered anyone.

Apparently, such people don't need grace.

Yet—they do. Because here's the rub for everyone: Jesus didn't nullify the Law. Quite the contrary. He said He'd come to fulfil it and not the tiniest part would be overturned. Grace does not negate Law. In fact, Jesus' attitude to the Law of Moses was that it's the minimum requirement, not a maximum. His followers are actually expected to do better.

God's grace never includes tolerance for shabby behaviour—grace is not His forgiveness for treating others in a way we would hope they would never treat us, simply because He looks at us through lenses coloured with the blood of Jesus.

The Law of Moses said: don't commit adultery. Jesus said: don't even lust because that's adultery of the heart.

The Law of Moses said: don't kill. Jesus said: don't even be angry because that's murder of the heart.

Jesus took the Law of Moses and raised it to an unimaginable degree.

The Law of Moses said: don't steal. Jesus said: sell what you have and give the money to the poor.

The Law of Moses said: Honour your father and mother. Jesus said: treat everyone around you as if they were your mother and father and brothers and sisters and therefore worthy of the same high honour.

This is the purpose of grace: to empower the believer beyond the minimum requirements of the Law; to give us the ability to obey the surpassingly high commands of Jesus; to shower us with the authority and responsibility to obey the principles behind the Law—love of God and love of neighbour—with faithfulness and honour.

Grace does not supersede the Law but rather transcends it. Grace doesn't make the Law less in the sense that it becomes optional, it makes it less in the sense that there's an even higher command to obey.

Throughout the New Testament, grace is considered to be variegated, multi-coloured, rainbow-hued. This makes sense because it is an empowerment to acquire all the fruits and virtues: love, joy, peace, patience, kindness, goodness, gentleness, faithfulness, self-control, mercy, truthfulness, justice, righteousness, integrity, honour, gratitude, generosity, responsibility, holiness, endurance.

These are the things against which there is no law.

Yet, 'grace' has become an excuse for some of us—a pretext for doing nothing about our own acts of injustice, violence, dishonesty, infidelity, callousness. When we forego the kiss of justice, peace, truth and mercy, we not only divest ourselves of God's armour but we demean His glory and present it to those around us as a tawdry, hypocritical thing.

Grace is empowerment to achieve the impossible.

When a husband cheats on his wife, it's the power for the wife to forgive, the husband to repent and the church to discipline in love and right order.

Too often the church tosses the problem in the 'too hard' basket and simply pressures the woman to forgive. Thereby adding abuse to the situation, not grace.

Reconciliation is a two-way street. And because reconciliation is about relationship, it requires two responses, not one. Whether it's about a husband forgiving a wife, an employee forgiving a workplace bully, a contractor forgiving a client ignoring calls for payment or a friend forgiving a theft or insult, a re-activated relationship requires a response. Sure, on one side is forgiveness. And on the other, repentance and, where possible, restitution.

Grace empowers both.

Forgiveness by itself does not restore relationship.

God's forgiveness is always available, always held out to erring humanity, but by itself, it does not constitute a relationship. We have to respond to the covenant He holds out to us. Even though we can't manage something as simple as that.

Grace is necessary to empower even our response.

Only in returning to Me and resting in Me will you be saved.

Isaiah 30:15 NLT

Grace transcends the Law; not, as is so often understood, by by-passing it but by offering the power to superabundantly fulfil it. Sometimes we can look at what Jesus says about loving your enemies instead of extracting an eye for an eye and a tooth for a tooth and see, in our own legislative-oriented minds, another Law. One that can cause us to despair with its impossible demands.

But grace should be as sweet and comforting as a father sweeping us up and carrying us on his shoulders when we realise that the mountain of the law is impossible to climb. As he ascends higher, he doesn't expect us to jump off into every mud pool or a lava pit by the wayside—just so he can rescue us. Our job is to hold onto him.

Grace is therefore never the liberty to perpetuate injustice, refuse to grant mercy, deal falsely or sow discord. God is the Potter who kisses His Bride with mercy, justice, truth and peace and thereby armours us against the attacks of the Enemy.

Grace is the empowerment of the Holy Spirit to forgive betrayal at the deepest level.

Grace never says, 'It doesn't matter.' Grace never excuses. Never abuses. Never tolerates. Never rationalises. Never minimises. Never exonerates. Never accepts a plea bargain or a self-serving technicality in defence.

Which—terrifyingly—is what many Christians today believe about the God they serve. They envisage the Judge of the Universe as less interested in faithfulness as in a single moment of faith involving baptism or a prayer asking Jesus into our lives. Never mind whether this invitation is the right way around or not: we're appalled at judges who let thieves, murderers or paedophiles off on legal technicalities, yet don't blink at the idea of a God more interested in legal niceties than in genuine justice.

Is this what Paul meant by 'grace'? Unconditional acceptance of unrepentant betrayal? When a man abuses his wife, grace might empower her to work through forgiveness but grace does not require her to remain in harm's way.

'God has forgiven him outright; why can't you?' the church often asks, thereby throwing in a guilt trip and exacerbating the abuse.

Forgiveness—and its companion virtue, mercy—are gods in many congregations. There's a huge chasm between 'God is love' and 'Love is God', between 'God is merciful' and 'Mercy is God', between 'God is just' and 'Justice is God'.

Grace judges, just as the Lord of Grace does. That might be surprising—but to do anything less is to justify the sin and not the sinner.

In judging, grace acknowledges the pain, the hurt, the wounding—the disruption of relationship that sin causes—and then, grace enables the process of forgiveness to begin. Because grace also acknowledges that relationship is the most important of all.

Grace judges—yes, that's true—but grace also loves. Grace is merciful.

But it does not turn forgiveness into a god.

Is God's forgiveness unlimited? When Peter queried Jesus about how many times we should forgive someone who asks, He gave a very specific, finite number. We've turned this into an indefinite—indeed, infinite—number by suggesting that seventy (or seventy times seven, depending on the translation) isn't meant to be understood as a precise figure.

Yet the testimony of Scripture suggests otherwise. God is slow to anger, incredibly patient, always ready to forgive and ever ready to empower our repentance, but nowhere does it suggest He is infinitely tolerant. Both 70 and 490 are recorded in reference to the limitation of His forbearance.

Jeremiah 25:11-12 prophesies that the people of Judah will be captives of the Babylonians for seventy years. Daniel, living in exile at the end of that period, recalls the prophecy[65] when Darius came to power and, in his prayer to God, confesses that, for 490 years, the people did not allow the land to rest every seventh year. God gave the land its accumulated rest (as per the statute of Leviticus 26:43), through the enforced exile of the people.

Here we see God allowing 490 years for repentance—not unlimited time.

Jesus, however, was probably not referencing the Babylonian exile when He answered Peter's question. He was probably alluding to the most ancient act of unrepentant arrogance on record.

Cain had murdered Abel—and was sorry for it, if for no other reason than that his punishment was greater than he could bear. (Some ancient sources say he said his crime was 'too great to be forgiven!') God, in His mercy, gave Cain a mark to protect him and promised him he would be avenged sevenfold, if he were killed. This proved sufficient deterrent for five or six generations.

Cain's great-great-great grandson, Lamech, turned God's hedge of protection into a thornbed of unbridled vengeance. Lamech told his wives he'd killed a young man in retaliation for a bruise. He stated that if anyone tried to exact retribution—well, Cain might be avenged seven times—but Lamech would be avenged seventy times (or seventy times seven, again depending on the translation.)

Jesus turned Lamech's curse on its head. Bless, instead of avenge. Forgive a hit or a bruise, don't repay it with murder.

His answer to Peter's question is really: 'Be like God. Patient. Loving. Forgiving.'

But forgiving does not mean forgoing justice. It does not mean forfeiting restitution. It does not mean repentance is optional. It does not mean we should accept abuse.

Because the purpose of grace is for reconciliation: between God and ourselves; between ourselves and others.

In forgiving, we give up our expectations and our right to put conditions on the restoration of relationship. In making restitution where we have wronged others, we should equally give up our expectations that trust will be immediately restored and forgiveness flow automatically.

Paradoxically, where grace is present, we should be able to expect all this—in time. Yet, when only one person in the relationship is empowered by grace, hard decisions may need to be made. Separation may be required; for the same reason that it's wise to cut off a gangrenous limb from an otherwise healthy body. We have to remember we are part of the Body—vitally and seamlessly integrated—not a set of interconnected individuals. While we may admire maverick heroes, they're not God's calling for anyone. The rugged individualism lionised by a previous generation allowed the rise of narcissism as a virtue just two generations later.

Narcissism—obsessive self-love—is the enemy of grace.

And it's no coincidence that its current rise is fuelled by Facebook—a social platform that began as an act of vengeance against a girlfriend.

Each generation wants new symbols, new people, new names. They want to divorce themselves from their predecessors.

Jim Morrison

RR Reno writes about attending a synagogue with his Jewish wife and having to resist the 'reductive caricature' Christians have about so-called Jewish legalism. The rabbis consider that at Rosh Hashanah—the Feast of Trumpets, the beginning of the civil year—God opens the books of life and writes the names of His chosen people in it.[66] Some are appointed to live, some to die, some to have good lives, some bad. During the next ten days, until Yom Kippur—the Day of Atonement—prayer, fasting and good deeds can change this divine decree. At the end of that time, the books of life are shut.

Reno points out that many Christians see Judaism through the lens of the Pharisees of the first century and imagine the book of life to be like a bank account with good deeds deposited here or there. It's seen as the antithesis of grace; as an attempt to earn salvation. 'Jews, we think, are legalistic, engaged in a tit-for-tat relationship with God, spirituality based on external commandments rather than one that encourages us to commune with Him in an intimate, spiritual way.'

Yet his experience shows this is a simplistic view. He finds himself 'encountering a God who looms above as the very Author of all things, the arbiter of life and death, and the awesome judge of men—and the God who opens Himself to human influence, draws near to see our gestures, hear our prayers, and heed our petitions. I've felt this tense spiritual atmosphere of divine transcendence *and* intimacy with an especial power on Yom Kippur.'

The first service on the evening of the Day of Atonement is known as Kol Nidre, *all vows*. It opens with a solemn call for a court, both in heaven and on earth, to come into session. A petition is then put forward, asking the court for release from all future vows, promises and pledges.

As Reno points out, this is 'conceptually odd'. How can anyone make a promise in the future if they've already petitioned in advance for it not to be considered a promise? Kol Nidre is traditionally understood to refer only to vows made to God. But in some ways that makes it worse. Isn't it a conflict of interest to ask God never to hold us to account for any promises we make to Him, or before Him?

This peculiar petition, presented in a courtroom context, is delivered through a heart-rending chant. Legal language is entirely absent; instead the music is full of deep and desperate pleas.

Reno interprets the paradox, suggesting that the cantor and congregation are effectively acknowledging, 'O Lord, I am a precipitous, presumptuous, impetuous fool. Please see that my eager spiritual efforts in the year to come are as likely to be motivated by vanity as obedience, by self-interest as devotion.'

Yom Kippur ends with a service known as Ne'ilah, *closing the gate*. The doors to the sanctuary that hold the Torah scrolls are opened and, for an hour, the congregation stands as the service circles through a single theme: 'The doors are closing, the doors are closing.'

'The shadows lengthen. The half-light of impeding darkness gathers around the synagogue. The atmosphere becomes urgent. God, our Lord and Judge, beckons us to repent, but not forever. Death is nearer than we think. Time is short. The doors are closing... Grace abounds, but as modern Christians I fear that we presume upon God's mercy. Jesus issued a dire warning to those of us who imagine that we can tarry, putting off the real changes required by true repentance until after we get our worldly lives in order: "No one who puts his hand to the plough and looks back is fit for the kingdom of God." I should be casting aside the luggage of life and running to enter the kingdom of God. I strain, I desire to purify my soul. But I take my hand off the plough. I look back. I am Christian... I have no real grasp of Hebrew and I only vaguely follow the prayers in my wife's synagogue. Yet, in the final moments of Yom Kippur I have felt a terrible anguish, yearning to move, and yet immobile, wanting to rush to God's side and yet nailed to my worldly life. I have shuddered as cantor cries out: "The doors are closing; the doors are closing." For in those haunting words I hear Jesus saying: "Repent, for the Kingdom of God is at hand."'[67]

Repent...

Because repentance is about clearing the ground for restoring relationship. How on earth did we come to see it as a legalism, opposed to grace?

Grace has become, for some believers, the religious equivalent of a shame-eraser. While secular society has worked hard to redefine shame so that it's all about getting caught out for cheating, rather than for the act of cheating itself, the Christian world has been busily redefining shame too. We've always been able to sponge it away through the blood of Jesus but now many people ignore the plain words of Paul. The deeper we are in sin, the more grace abounds—but that, he clearly says, is no reason to go out and sin more.

Yet, for some people, grace has become an excuse for deliberate and unrepentant sin: for betrayal in business, for betrayal of a spouse, for betrayal of friends, for betrayal of workmates, for betrayal of children.

Grace is no longer seen as an empowerment to turn away from sin—the deeper the sin, the greater the empowerment—but rather as a technical point of law, which allows us a free pass to salvation. This means that, for many people, they feel they no longer have to struggle against temptation. For them, it doesn't really matter one way or another. What Jesus has done on the cross covers their sin, past and future. Once saved, God's grace sees the righteousness of Jesus, not the infidelity, the betrayal, the dishonesty or the indifference.

The idea is lost that we are covered by Jesus' righteousness and also called into it so that our lives become a window to His holiness. The idea we could bring dishonour to the name of God is nowhere to be seen.

This clever ploy of the satan to redefine grace in the Christian sphere brings with it a redefinition of shame.

Just as in society at large 'getting caught' at fraud is the new high crime, not the theft itself, in Christian circles 'unforgiveness' is the new high sin. Shame is projected at the one sinned against far more often than it is against the one sinning. We've defined the sin of the older brother in the story of the Prodigal Son as much more serious than the one of younger brother.

It's the old, old story. Adam blamed Eve; Eve blamed the serpent. We're always looking for someone else to blame and shame. Now we've institutionalised it even in our mode of understanding Jesus' stories and Paul's letters.

We fail to understand we're up against spiritual powers who can use even the grace of God against us.

I've been studying threshold covenants for years now. At first, the only guide I had was Henry Clay Trumball's *The Threshold Covenant* and the experiences of a small group of women willing to pray for each other. While several people have now written or spoken about them, I don't know of anyone else gathering empirical evidence about the modus operandi of the cosmic powers on the threshold.

In *God's Pageantry*, I mentioned three guardians. If all is well, then two holy cherubim and an unfallen seraph will be watching your own personal threshold for you. If it isn't well, then Python, Rachab and Leviathan will be waiting.

Scripture recognises the association between Python and the threshold. English translations do not differentiate between 'kaph' and 'miphtan', both meaning *threshold*. The latter is derived from 'pethen', *twisting snake*, and is a possible origin of English *python*. A close examination of 'miphtan', however, shows it is used for a defiled threshold.

Other spirits lurk there too.

At first encounter, they seemed new, scary and strange to me and my prayer partners. But there came a moment of recognition when we realised we'd known it for as long as we could remember. Such spirits include one I've dubbed the 'Janissary Spirit', which works in consort with a vampire spirit.

We see the Janissary spirit operating in such stories as the Prodigal Son when the younger son goes to the father and asks for his inheritance. In effect, he says to his dad: 'I wish you were dead.'

This epitomises the function of the Janissary spirit: to train up a child to murder the father.

The word 'Janissary' is taken from the troops of the Old Ottoman Empire. Young boys were taken from Christian families as a levy, indoctrinated into a new religion, trained as an elite fighting force loyal to the Sultan, then sent out against, among others, their own people. A diabolically ingenious concept, militarily speaking: your forces are brainwashed into being so utterly loyal they will fight to the death for you, but they're also totally expendable because they're not your own people. Although 'Janissary' is Old Turkish for 'new troops', the association of the name over many centuries with guarding the Sublime Porte—an entrance and doorway which symbolised the empire as a whole—is one of several aspects giving it threshold overtones.

Janissaries existed from the fourteenth century to the early nineteenth century—a period of five hundred years. The concept was revived by Islamic State who took Yazidi boys and trained them as 'cubs of the caliphate' to fight against their own people.

Janissaries operated for such a long period they exerted an immensely strong influence on the psyche of the Ottoman people: resulting, I believe, in the expectation that their enemies would give them the resources to do their fighting for them.

As I write this section, revelations have rocked America that, at the time of the fatal attack on the US embassy in Benghazi in 2012, the US military establishment was running guns from Benghazi to Syria—effectively empowering the rise of Islamic State. A decade ago, a similar situation resourced the Taliban. A century ago, in early 1915, the failure of the British navy to get through the straits of the Dardanelles with the accompanying loss of so many ships led to the disastrous campaign at Gallipoli. And just why was Britain, then 'mistress of the seas', unable to overcome Turkish defences? Because Britain gave the Ottoman Empire the very sea mines used against them and because, until just a few months prior to Gallipoli, Britain was still helping Turkey modernise its army and navy.

As we look around the world today, we see the fingerprints of the Janissary spirit at work. They're everywhere—from the conflicts raging across the Middle East and central Africa, to the biased reporting of journalists on religious persecution, to the removal of parental rights in our education systems.

How do we discern this spirit at work in society? Its hallmarks are:
- a fighting force is created from the enemy's children; they are trained to believe differently and to oppose their own people
- the enemy resources the fight against itself—physically through the gifting of weapons or personnel, intellectually through propaganda against itself and its allies, spiritually and emotionally through fear and intimidation
- the enemy's children are brought up to murder their parents or their parents' generation—not necessarily physically but

certainly when it comes to slaying ideas and beliefs. Already in Canada, the USA and other parts of the western world, basic freedoms have been stripped from parents. Here in Australia in some states, it is illegal for a teacher to give a girl an aspirin without parental approval but perfectly lawful to refer her to a doctor for an abortion without their knowledge or consent. When family groups have tried to lodge a complaint on a government website about brochures being given to children in schools, they have been refused because the quote from the brochure is obscene! Yet it is lawful to put this same brochure with the obscene quote into the hands of students of primary school age.

- surprise attack to stun observers into silence as well as to immobilise them. By the time the shock and disbelief wears off, vital time and opportunity for re-grouping has been lost. Activists are currently at work across the western world to get laws changed so as to ensure the full force of government intervention and criminal law is at work to compel anyone who thinks differently into silence. The purpose of such bullying is to impose quiet acceptance of what children are being taught about sexuality, morality, ethics and religion.

In many ways, we might consider the Janissary spirit as the 'spirit of the age'. The rise of the vampire as hero in modern fiction is another indication of its upsurge.

How and why do the Janissary spirit and vampire spirit work together? Simple. The Janissary spirit wants to kill you but knows there's the strongest possibility that, since you are a Christian, you will come back to life spiritually through the resurrection power of Jesus. You might succumb to the twisted modern notions of hypergrace. However, chances are, even then that the Holy Spirit may use the gifts of guilt and shame to convict you of sin and bring you back into the sheepfold of Jesus.

This is where the vampire spirit comes in. It wants to feed off that resurrection power. It's a spirit that stabs, stakes and pierces: it knows full well that the piercing of Jesus on the Cross brought about new birth.

It wants to siphon off that power by piercing you.

And because blood and spirit are connected,[68] a vampire spirit can feed on spirit as well as blood. Like the younger brother in the story of the Prodigal Son, it wants your inheritance as a child of God.

In my early twenties, I was thrilled when my boyfriend asked me to marry him. It had been a rocky courtship and, due to family differences, we'd broken off our relationship for a while and he'd been going out with someone else. He assured me all had been ironed out with his family and he'd realised I was the one girl for him.

At the time I was teaching in a rural area out west and he was working up north. We made plans to get together and announce our engagement at a simple morning tea at church six weeks later. We'd make it over into a surprise engagement party. Because of the distance between us, that month's phone bill was huge. Every time we signed off for the night, I asked him again if everything was truly sorted out with his family and I gave him the opportunity to back out of the engagement before we went public. Every time, he reassured me the problems were over.

Still the surprise party turned out to be much more of a surprise than I could ever have anticipated. Because my fiancé got up and announced his engagement to someone else.

I was shattered. I felt as if someone had dashed me against a rock and broken me into pieces. He seemed startled at how devastated I was.

I kept asking myself how I had missed realising what was going on. Did I really give him dozens of opportunities to back out gracefully or did I only imagine I did? What signs were there that this was going to happen?

Over the subsequent decades, this was a question I asked myself often. More often than not when there was a threshold event in my life—not that I would have termed them that way for many years—I would be wounded by a completely unexpected action by a friend or colleague. And I would berate myself as the most foolish woman on the planet. Foolish, because I had never learned to spot the signs that someone I thought I knew well was about to show an entirely different side to their character.

I couldn't even spot the signs when it came to observing other people approach a threshold. Several of my colleagues applied for an internal promotion: Head of Department in Mathematics. Each of the candidates would have been genuinely happy had the other received the nod. However all were in their early forties and all were turned down—off the record, of course—on the basis of their age. Instead the position was given to a twenty-five year-old outsider with no experience in management or teaching mathematics.

It quickly became evident this was a disastrous appointment. The principal had several options but took none of them. Instead she told the previous candidates for the position that they were to mentor the new Head of Department into the role for as long as required. If necessary, they were to do his work for him, rather than allow the students to suffer. Immense pressure was put on them to do a job they'd been told they were not the best person for—and to do it without extra pay or reward.

One resigned after a few months and the others all applied for transfers which, for years, were denied.

Watching this happen eventually caused me to articulate the idea of people being staked in place; impaled in a situation that sucks the life and vitality out of them. I used the words 'staked', 'spiked', 'impaled', 'nailed down' as descriptors for years before I ever thought to connect them with a vampire spirit on a threshold.

I did, however, have enough sense of having been pierced through myself that I eventually asked for prayer from a ministry group. I explained about the surprise engagement party and said I felt I was impaled to that moment. I asked for prayer to withdraw the stake pinning me to that time. I knew I couldn't get the stake out myself. It was too big. A few seconds into the prayer, the woman next to me started screaming. The leader stopped and calmly explained that this woman was voicing the pain I was not in touch with.

Many secular and spiritual counsellors insist on getting in touch with the pain, in going back to fill out the memory or bring it up out of repression. I don't believe in that. I'm a huge advocate of **not** going where the pain is so deep that it feels as though it will kill you if you stop detaching from it. Prayer can be surgical and gentle at the same time. It doesn't have to probe too deeply to be effective.

And it can heal the wounds inflicted during even the worst surprise attack of the Janissary spirit and its ally, the vampire who pins us down in order to feed off our resurrection life.

Just a few months after receiving prayer for removal of the stake, I was able to bless someone else the same way. And I've repeated it many times since.

When I finally passed my own threshold—and I still wasn't able to see any warning signs that someone was about to do something that would feel as if I was staked, yet again, to their threshold, I went to God in a lament. I still wasn't learning from my past mistakes.

And I felt that God said this to me: the reason I don't see any signs is because *there are none*.

It doesn't matter how long you've known a person or how well you think you know them. The threshold is a unique place. You won't know if it's a 'miphtan' or a 'kaph'—defiled or not—until the moment you reach it. The person I am as I step over the threshold cannot be predicted by the person I was even one second prior.

It's impossible to predict whether, on the first approach to the threshold into destiny, I am going to turn out to be a person who sacrifices myself to the threshold guardians. Or whether I am in reality a person who sacrifices other people to them so I can pass relatively unscathed. Or whether I am a person who, on sensing their presence, flees in fear. Or whether I am a person who truly believes Jesus is the all-sufficient sacrifice for every threshold.

The heart is deceitful and wicked above all things, says Jeremiah, and what is in our hearts doesn't become evident until this unique moment. All thresholds require a sacrifice. Even the threshold into destiny—into that true calling prophesied in the name God breathed over us when we were conceived.

What are we willing to sacrifice to achieve our true destiny? We can't know the answer to that question until we reach the threshold and discover whether we are armoured in God's panoply or not.

Whether we've sacrificed others or sacrificed ourselves, we are complicit with the dark threshold spirits and have been faithless to God. If we've fled from the threshold instead, we've also been faithless. Yet we should be encouraged by 2 Timothy 2:11–13 NKJV:

…if we died with Him, we shall also live with Him.
If we endure, we shall also reign with Him.
If we deny Him, He also will deny us.
If we are faithless, He remains faithful; He cannot deny Himself.

Scripture is the touchstone when it comes to identifying spirits of the threshold. And I don't mind admitting that it's impossible to find the Janissary spirit or the vampire spirit mentioned there. At least under those particular names. Scripture does, however, describe a scene where these two spirits seem to be at work—and, if anyone were to insist on Biblical terminology, then perhaps we could call them the 'spirits of Helkath-hazzurim'.

Let's look at a bizarre and tragic event early in the reign of King David, not long after the death of Saul.

David's nephew, Joab, was the commander of his armies. Saul's nephew, Abner, was the commander of the former king's armies and initially didn't support David. Instead he threw his military might behind one of Saul's surviving sons. This was a time when there were effectively two kings, each vying for supremacy.

Peculiarly, Joab and Abner seem to have been friends, even if on opposing sides. One day they met at the Pool of Gibeon. Each had a band of troops with them and they all sat, staring at each other, across the expanse of water.

Now what happened next is so disturbing that invariably translators of 2 Samuel 2:14 have trouble interpreting the text. Most versions have Abner proposing a fight. I am indebted to Arie Uittenbogaard who points out that Abner actually suggests to Joab that they have the men provide a 'laugh'—the verb used comes from 'shaq', *laugh*, as in the name Isaac. Twelve men from David's side and twelve from the tribe of Benjamin are chosen. They pair off and proceed to grab each other by the hair while stabbing each other in the side. And, not unnaturally, all of them fall down dead.

Now perhaps Joab and Abner found this amusing but it seems the rest of the troops didn't get the joke. A skirmish broke out with one side attacking the other. In the middle of the ruckus, Abner slipped quietly away.

However he was seen. Joab's brother Asahel took off after him. Asahel was reputedly as swift as a wild gazelle. He pursued Abner relentlessly and Abner, realising it was his friend's brother who was following him, repeatedly tried to get him to turn back. When Asahel refused, Abner thrust a spear through him and impaled him to the ground.

There's a lot more to the story but this is the crux of the matter as far as the Janissary and vampire spirits go. Now, as Arie Uittenbogaard says, the attitude of the two commanders is maniacal and David's response when it's all over is bizarre. There are also deeply suggestive overtones to the numerics of twelve men from each side but the meaning behind their suicidal game is just plain elusive. The name given to the place where this lunatic event takes place is Helkath-hazzurim which, because it's so difficult to translate, unfortunately doesn't shed much light on its significance.[69]

However, as I have pointed out in *God's Pageantry*, the element, *to laugh*, as it occurs in the name Isaac, has secondary meanings, most of which have threshold overtones. In Hebrew 'shaq' also means *lintel*, and is related to *watchful* as well as having a resonance of *to be wakeful*. In Turkish, it has actually come down to us as *threshold*.[70]

In addition, covenant violation lurks in the background of this story. The location for the suicidal sport proposed by Abner is the Pool of Gibeon. The significance of this is not pointed out within this story—and only becomes apparent nineteen chapters later when it is revealed Gibeon had been the site of a genocidal massacre. Saul, before he had died in battle, had all but wiped out the people of Gibeon, breaking the covenant that had been cut with them centuries before when Joshua first crossed the Jordan. Saul's blood-letting was to have devastating consequences for the land and people much later in David's reign. However, largely unnoticed, Saul's action actually repeated the pattern of genocidal massacre which had occurred in his own hometown, Gibeah of Benjamin, in a previous generation.

When we look deeply into this incident and note that Asahel's body was taken home to be buried in Bethlehem, we see a conflict that had endured for generations between individuals in Gibeah and individuals in Bethlehem. It's a struggle that had, from time to time, become full-on tribal warfare. It had all started back in the time of the Judges with threshold covenant violation and the death of a woman from Bethlehem.

However we can also see the vampire and Janissary spirits at work here. The mark of the Janissary spirit is the desire to kill the father—and each of the twelve men chosen for the suicidal game are, in fact, killing representatives of the father. Joab and Abner each have 'ab', *father*, as part of their name.

Both these spirits are threshold spirits. The threshold nature of this incident is indicated by Abner's call for a 'laugh'—a word that could just have easily been translated as 'threshold' or 'game' or both.

This makes me wonder about laughter yoga. Yoga means *yoked*—in the sense, *yoked to a spirit*. The yoga spirit, 'kundalini', is invariably described as python-like, however there's no reason why Python could not deputise the Janissary spirit for exercises involving laughter.

Abner kills Asahel in a vampire-like way: by impalement. Asahel means *created by God* and his death describes exactly what the vampire spirit wants to do to those re-created by God through the new birth. To take life from them; to suck their destiny away.

Whether we call these threshold spirits 'vampire' and 'Janissary' or 'spirits of Helkath-hazzurim', their defilement is the same. They want to bleed away your resurrection life and suck off your new birth so that, sooner or later, you turn away from your destiny in Christ.

How do we defend ourselves against them? One of their special targets, I am advised, is anyone who happens to have survived an abortion attempt by their mother.

The daggers and spears they wield on the threshold are the same as the darts of the evil one mentioned by Paul in Ephesians 6:16. We know this because, in discussing the Armour of God needed to pass over into our calling, he uses the Greek word 'belos', *darts*, which also happens to mean *threshold*.

Like the threshold stabbing game at Helkath Hazzurim, this is the satan's threshold jabbing sport.

The answer is simple. To protect ourselves, we put on the Armour of God and stand back-to-back with our Paraclete. And we don Christ's armour simply by asking for His kiss.

When we first respond to God, when we repent and place our faith in Him, we arrive at the moment of salvation. A transfer of ownership occurs. We like to say we are saved by faith, but that's not really true.

We are saved *by grace* through faith.

We are such dirty, chipped pots—sometimes we're broken so badly we're just shards of baked clay—that it's impossible for us to have faith of our own accord. Yet the grace of the Master Potter prevails. Once we turn to Him, we can never be taken out of His hand.

Still we need to be scrubbed cleaned, patched up, painted, put back together. As Bob Gass says, 'You're perfectly acceptable, if not yet acceptably perfect.' So we need to 'work out our salvation in fear and trembling'—that is, although our salvation is never in doubt because we can never be taken from the Potter's hand, we are asked to cooperate with Him in the process of sanctification. That's the cleaning up and putting-back-together phase.

Unlike those terracotta warriors at Mount Li as they are painstakingly restored, we have a choice. We can advance the restoration of ourselves or decide to turn away from it. Not that we do the work—that's God's place.

When we choose to allow God to accomplish forgiveness through us, we advance our own restoration. Notice: I didn't say 'when we choose to forgive.' All we can do is ask God to open the doors in us to allow His forgiveness to flow to others.

When we choose repentance, we advance our own restoration. Notice: I didn't say 'when we repent.' All we can do is ask God to open the doors in us to allow His power to enable us to turn away from our sins.

When we choose to renounce the way we have dishonoured others, we advance our own restoration. Notice: I didn't say 'when we stop dishonouring others.' All we can do is ask God to open the doors in us to allow His grace free access so that we naturally honour others.

Honour is a very difficult issue: according to Jude 1:8, we need to be careful in this regard, even with the satan. We cannot slander him. Nothing in God's creation, not even the fallen angels, can be dishonoured without consequence.

Slander and shame are tools of the Enemy. As mentioned previously, the very word for the satan in Greek, 'diabolos' (John 6:70), has the sense of both *slanderer* and *adversary*.[71]

The primary targets of slander and shame are our names and, through them, our identities and destinies.

Jesus exposed Himself to both slander and shame so that we need not lose ourselves to them ever again. He made the new covenant in His blood available to us so that, by becoming one with Him as His bride, His righteousness would be ours.

Abram was 86 years old when God cut a blood covenant with him. He was asleep at the time—an image of us, dead in our sins, when Jesus cuts the new covenant in His blood with us.

Abram was almost 100 years old when God appeared to Him and instituted a name covenant, giving him the name Abraham. Six days later, God appeared with two angels, accepted Abraham's hospitality and, with it, both threshold and salt covenants. For all of these events, Abraham was awake.

Likewise, while it is wholly God's action to provide a blood covenant for us while we are still asleep in our sins, it is while we are awake in grace that He wants us to partner with Him in at least three other covenants. The natural timing of these other covenants is fourteen years after we were first saved.

The first seven of those fourteen years is meant to be spent in battle. Like Joshua's conquest of the Promised Land, the first seven years is about taking down spiritual strongholds in our lives, battling to overcome addictions (and therefore the shame at the root of them), clearing out the Enemy within. The second seven of those fourteen years is more restful—it's about colonising the newly-cleansed landscape of our souls, restoring and repopulating our thoughts with new towers and cities that are built by the Presence of God Himself. Of course, we may—like Caleb—have a few tenacious giants still to clear off. Giants occupying an old family place of name and threshold covenant and who do not want us to come into a deeper relationship with the living God.

Now the satan is fully aware of the natural timing for these last three covenants. And he'll throw everything he can at us in the thirteenth year to get us to trade with him when it comes to the name covenant. The closer we get to a threshold covenant, the more he'll direct his agents—Python, the spirit of constriction, and Rachab, the spirit of wasting—to pile the pressure on. And should, by some miracle of grace, we actually pass over the threshold, he'll instruct Leviathan, the spirit of backlash, to find some area of dishonour in our lives that will give a legal right to whiplash us right back the other way.

Take a moment to think about your Christian experience, if you've been a follower of Jesus for more than fourteen years. What happened in the thirteenth year?

I discovered this fourteen year cycle as a result of noticing an attempt to create a threshold covenant by the satan as a beachhead for taking over another country. My first reaction was to complain to God that He'd sent me to pray for this particular nation fourteen years too late. But, as God led me into looking deeper into blood covenants and threshold covenants, I noted the fourteen year gap in the stories of Abraham and of Joshua. And then I sensed God say to me: 'I didn't send you fourteen years too late. There are seventeen days left until the time is up.'

In shock, I realised the reason the Enemy followed the biblical pattern is because he can't create anything of his own. Even to despoil, he is forced to adhere to God's blueprints.

Over time, I started to think about my own experience. I became a Christian when I was six in the week before Easter. It was a spontaneous reaction on listening to my classroom teacher tell the story of the Last Supper and Jesus' death and resurrection. Fourteen years later came that time around my surprise engagement which was so devastating, I felt my personality was shattered. In retrospect, now I know about threshold covenants, I also feel I was 'staked' to that threshold as a sacrifice.

It took me about thirteen years to recover sufficiently to get my life back on track. And then, as the fourteenth year approached, another disaster rocked my world. And thirteen years after that...

Well, God suggested, with the strongest possible hints, I leave my home country for a year. I look back now and I wonder what He was protecting me from. I certainly wasn't anywhere near my destiny but the pattern was broken for long enough for me to rest. Well, maybe not so much 'rest', as 'be arrested' on the path to more damage.

And, as I paused, I had time to become curious about a phenomenon

I began to notice in my reading: why were so many authors intent on redefining their names? Why were so many writers engaged in the literary equivalent of Jacob's struggle with the angel at the ford of Jabbok?

God had my attention. I'd always had a quiet interest in names. And eventually, as that interest was fanned into a passion, it became clear I was observing a name covenant. From there, over the course of several years, my enquiries inevitably led to covenant perversion—the covenant with death—and, in short order, to threshold or cornerstone covenants.

It quickly became evident very few people had even heard of these. Yet hundreds of authors were struggling, all unknowingly, with name covenants. Choosing to devote enormous time and energy to the conflict.

Something was obviously very wrong. And as I began to talk with people about constriction and wasting in preparation for *God's Pageantry*, I realised that name and threshold covenants might well be the elephant in the room that we never discuss.

It wasn't just *my* problem. Not by a long shot.

Long before God cut a blood covenant with Abram, they were in relationship together. It just wasn't a covenantal one. When he was 75, God directed Abram to leave his father's house in Haran and head for Canaan. Eleven years later their friendship deepened through cutting a blood covenant. Then, fourteen years after that, their intimacy consolidated over the course of six days through name, threshold and salt covenants.

A relationship with God isn't necessarily a covenant.

For at least two years before they exchanged names, Simon and Jesus were in relationship together. The frank easiness of their friendship is evident in many interchanges. But again their relationship wasn't a covenantal one until that climactic moment at Caesarea Philippi.

Similarly the other disciples were in varying degrees of relationship with Jesus. They followed Jesus around for three years, in close companionship with Him. But it wasn't until the Last Supper that, Judas excluded, they came into covenantal oneness with Him.

Modern Christianity tends to assume that anyone in relationship with Jesus is in covenant. But is this true?

Is your relationship with Jesus an acquaintanceship or a covenant? Which of blood, name, threshold and salt covenants have you undertaken?

Perhaps it's time to ask Him if He's waiting for you to approach Him about the last three. The first is His alone to initiate but the others may well be yours.

From antiquity, people have recognised the connection between naming and power.

Casey Miller and Kate Swift

There's one occasion in life when many people—quite by accident—take up the sword of the Spirit against Python just as it's about to strike. We call 1 Corinthians 13 the 'love chapter' and tend to wield it, almost indiscriminately, during wedding ceremonies. But this passage is not actually about romantic love or marriage or even covenant. It's about how to deal with Python.

The Corinthians lived in a licentious city on the Bay of Corinth—just across the waters from one of the most famous temples of ancient times: Delphi. There the temple of Apollo sat high on cliffs above the bay. Worshippers came from all over the ancient world, seeking advice from Python Apollo, the spirit of divination.

Paul encountered this spirit at Philippi: a slave girl would follow him and proclaim that he brought news about the living God. Paul rounded on her, cast out the Python spirit and then got into serious trouble with the law because her masters had been exploiting her ability to prophesy. (Acts 16:19)

Likewise, at Delphi, the priests of the sanctuary were engaged in profiteering. The sibyl—'Pythoness'—who delivered the prophetic statements didn't charge for being questioned. But the priests of Apollo made a very tidy sum by interpreting her answers. The Pythoness would sit in a cave on a brass tripod placed over a fissure from which noxious fumes emanated. She'd chew laurel leaves and babble her prophecies in a strange tongue or a riddling statement.

Croesus, a king famed for his wealth, came inquiring about an invasion he was considering. He later wanted to sue the Delphic oracle over the outcome but it was pointed out he'd simply failed to recognise the ambiguity in the statement: 'If Croesus attacks, a great empire will be destroyed.'

Humbler men than Croesus came asking about possible trade ventures or marriage partners, suitable crops or the best time to plant. Nero, before he became emperor of Rome, came and took away about six hundred fine marble statues. The loss hardly made a dent in the collection. He also asked about one of Delphi's great mysteries. An 'E' was carved on the navelstone and prominently displayed elsewhere. He inquired what it meant, but didn't get an answer.

Plutarch, later to become the high priest, discussed Nero's question with friends. It wasn't that the answer was a secret; it was simply that no one knew. The meaning of the 'E' had been lost in the mists of time. Plutarch's two best guesses were that it was an ancient Greek abbreviation for 'if', *ei*, or else it came from the verb form, *eimai*, a part of 'to be' or 'to exist' in the phrase *ego eimai*, 'I am'.

To justify his opinion, he pointed out that the questions to the Pythoness often began with 'if'; her answers also often began with 'if'. 'If' was fundamentally about choice.

If.
I am.

Look how often Paul uses 'if' and 'I am' in the thirteenth chapter of his epistle to the Corinthians. He also alludes to other aspects of the rites of Python Apollo, such as speech in other tongues, acquisition of wisdom and knowledge, prophesy and divination—making at least twelve references in just three verses.

*If I speak in the <u>tongues</u> of men and of angels, but have not love, **I am** only a <u>resounding gong</u> or a <u>clanging cymbal</u>. If I have the gift of <u>prophecy</u> and can fathom all <u>mysteries</u> and all <u>knowledge</u>, and **if** I have a faith that can move mountains, but have not love, **I am** nothing. If I give all I possess to the poor and surrender my body to the flames, but have not love, I gain nothing.*

1 Corinthians 13:1-3 NIV

Paul had reached the conclusion that love—agápē, *divine sacrificial love*—is the answer to the wiles of Python. No doubt in writing to the Corinthians and warning them about the tricks and schemes of this particular threshold guardian, he was also thinking about the Jewish understanding of 'if.'

The Hebrew word for *if* is 'eikev' which, like so many other Hebrew words we've encountered in this series, has more than one meaning. And of course, that second meaning is one so different we'd never suspect it. 'Eikev' also means *heel*. There is no reason to attach any significance to the fact that the word starts with the same letters as 'if' in Greek, because Hebrew has no vowels.

We find 'eikev' in names like Yaakov—which in English is *Jacob* and means *heel grasper* or *deceiver*. The sense of *heel* in Hebrew is entwined with the notion of *deceit*.

Yechiel Eckstein[72] connects the very first mention of *heel* in Scripture—God's curse of the serpent in Genesis 3:15—to the *'if'* in Moses' words recorded in Deuteronomy 7:12—

'I will put enmity between you and the woman, and between your offspring and hers; he will crush your head, and you will strike his **heel**.'

Genesis 3:15 NIV

'**If** *you pay attention to these laws and are careful to follow them, then the Lord your God will keep His covenant of love with you, as He swore to your ancestors.*'

Deuteronomy 7:12 TNIV

At first glance, these two verses don't seem in any way connected to each other. Yet they are both about choice.

What if we translated Genesis 3:15 as: '*he will crush your head, and you will strike his* **"if"**.'

In other words, every time we have a choice and say, 'If I...,' or 'If only...,' then Python has a legal right to be present. And that legal right goes back to the beginning of time and is based on God's promise.

From Deuteronomy 7:12, we then learn that God's covenant is dependent on keeping laws. However Paul later reveals that these are impossible to obey. But—nevertheless Jesus declared these laws are the absolute minimum God expects of us! That our righteousness must exceed that of the Pharisees! When the satan comes calling, our choices—our moments of *if*—must be based around sacrificial love. Or they're worth nothing.

Again, it's all about grace.

We can't achieve this through our own effort—only through God's covenant love. Because when we're in covenant with God, we're one with Him and that oneness enables His power to flow through us.

But when we're not one with Him—when, instead of a covenant with Him, we have a relationship—then Python is going to be crushing the life out of us by constricting all our choices. We should be crushing its head, but instead it's twisting every alternative path of 'if' we choose towards its own advantage.

The first time I ever read about the 'E' at Delphi was in the late 1990s in an essay by Guy Davenport. A few pages in *The Geography of the*

Imagination summarised Plutarch's conjectures and described the modern discovery of the navelstone by some archaeologists. My reaction to those pages was extraordinary.

To my own consternation, I immediately wrote a poem. I'd never done this before and I've never done it since: felt compelled to give voice to a poetic response. What I wrote disturbed me: my poem opened with exceptionally alliterative lines and powerful rhythms that flowed effortlessly out of me. After a page, the torrent stopped and the lines became a white-water churning of free verse. 'What provoked that?' I wondered when I finished.

At around the same time my sister rang me and asked me to interpret a dream.[73] She happened to ring just as I was nearing the end of the final edit of a children's fantasy I was writing. I was thinking about the next book in the series. 'What will I call it?' I wondered. 'What's the plotline?'

As she asked me what the dream meant, I had half my mind on my edits. She told me how, in the dream, she'd been an ancient entity who had come to his own ancestral house, looking for something, before leaving permanently and never returning. As the ancient entity, she'd met a caretaker who despised her, taken 'a set of drawers, beautifully carved and more ancient than history, a relic of the god Bel' and pushed them through a high open window, retrieved the item she came for and then, noticing a small pretty folding table high on a picture rail, decided it would be a very useful thing to have, so took it too.

'So,' my sister asks me, 'what is the meaning of what the ancient entity took?'

Thinking she was talking about the folding table, I breathed a sigh of relief and explained the symbolism.

But she wasn't talking about the table. What she was referring to was the item that the ancient entity, whom we surmised was actually a servant of the god Bel, had come looking for in the first place. 'Is there a god Bel?' she asked.

'Dunno,' I answered. 'What's this item he retrieved look like?'

'I have no idea,' my sister answered. 'I didn't see it.'

'You're asking me to identify this item and you've got no description of it? Is it big, or small? What's its size?'

'I don't know. I thought you might know.'

'Tell you what,' I said to her. 'I'll pray about this. I'm sure God will reveal the answer. But look—don't expect it quickly. Five weeks, maybe. Five months, more likely. Maybe even five years.'

We got off the phone and I returned to my editing. A title for the next book in the fantasy series flashed into my mind: 'Balthasar's Star.' *Now that's cool*, I thought. *The storyline could include the magi and the birth of Jesus.* My mind was bursting with possible storylines when I suddenly stopped. It dawned on me that, five years down the track, I wouldn't even remember I'd ever prayed about finding the answer to my sister's dream and wouldn't recognise it for what it was. I'd have forgotten I ever asked God to interpret it. So I prayed straight off that, in five years, I'd recognise the answer and remember I'd prayed.

Meantime I'd work on *Balthasar's Star*.

I was really glad five years later that I'd prayed about remembering and recognising. It took me all that time to realise that God had answered, not in five weeks or five months—or even five years— but in five seconds. Balthasar means *servant of the god, Bel*; it's the Babylonian name given to one of the two most famous dream interpreters in all of Scripture, the prophet Daniel. Moreover Daniel was twice appointed the leader of the magi—the mathematicians, astrologers and magicians who worked out the quadratic properties of five-pointed stars. However, this discovery is traditionally assigned to the Greek philosopher Pythagoras, who was named—as you may guess—after Python Apollo of Delphi.

Just as *Balthasar's Star* was ready for publication, my publisher went bankrupt. I should have been used to constriction by this stage of my life but I was still chafing at it. I really felt God had asked me to write this book about choices, the 'E' of Delphi, the cherubim, the mathematics of 'if', the golden ratio and a whole host of fantasy characters. I wasn't sure anyone would understand it; I certainly didn't. But I knew it had plumbed spiritual deeps greater than my own imagination. Although I'd created the mathematics of 'if' purely as a plot device which it was supposed to be as old as the magi and to have shown them the way to Bethlehem, I wanted the plot device to actually work. So when I'd finished the text, I set out all the calculations necessary to figure out how much mathematics I'd have to fudge to make it possible for a five-pointed star to really and truly direct the magi to Bethlehem. And, to my amazement, I found it didn't need any correction factor at all.

It was perfect.

It seemed, for a while, that was why God had used my sister's dream to give me the inspiration for the title of a children's novel. The story seemed useless in its own right but it served to help me understand how the golden ratio, God's universal signature, pointed the way to Bethlehem.

While writing *Balthasar's Star*, I began a serious investigation of names. I was gradually uncovering the concept of a name covenant. Not from the theoretical side but from an empirical angle: I observed that people acted as if they were struggling with myths that were connected to the origin of their names. And I noticed that the golden ratio in literature tended to be particularly prominent in the works of people whose names derived from Celtic 'Hugh' or 'Owen' or Teutonic 'Hesse'.

That baffled me. Why should a piece of mathematics be associated with any name, let alone these specific ones? Why them in particular? After considerable research I came across a statement by one of the brothers Grimm that these names might have a single origin in the old and incredibly savage Germanic god, Hesus. That immediately alarmed me. The name was too much like Jesus to be coincidental. And I'd been writing about the golden ratio too!

So I prayed straight off, as I've already testified in *God's Poetry*: 'Lord God, I have never ever deliberately prayed in the name of any god who might have usurped the name of Jesus of Nazareth, but *if* I have—*if* on any occasion ever I have unconsciously done so—then I repent and ask You to forgive me. And by the way, I pray this in the name of Jesus of Nazareth.'

As I finished, I saw in my mind's eye, a python rising out of my head. At the time, I didn't make the connection between the instances of emphatic '*if*' in my prayer and my vision of the exiting python. It took a few years for all of the jigsaw pieces to drop into place. Even when I had all the pieces, I didn't recognise some of them for what they were.

At one point I decided that, if all of this wasn't a product of a fevered imagination, but actually had some basis in spiritual reality, then 'if', 'I am', the 'golden ratio', and some sort of obscure allusion to the 'Delphic Oracle' should appear in Scripture. I am mortified to reveal that it took me more than six months to realise both how obvious and how well-known it was: the opening of 1 Corinthians 13.

Several more years went by. I was helping out in a small group at a prayer ministry training course when a woman asked for ministry for the effects of SRA—Satanic Ritual Abuse. She'd already received some ministry which, despite our ignorance and lack of experience with SRA, had gone very well. It had gone so well, in fact, the woman wanted more—and deeper. She described our faltering efforts to deal with a covenant with death and a name covenant as the best experience she'd had in twenty years of professional help.

'Right,' we said. 'Tell us the story of what you want more ministry for.'

'I can't.'

We explained how we did prayer ministry: 'tracking fruit to root', that is, tracing patterns through a person's life; looking at what events are making life unmanageable in the present and finding their source in the past. The ability to discern patterns is a skill many people have; when it is used in concert with the Holy Spirit's input, it is an aspect of prophecy.

The woman knew all this. 'I don't have anything I can tell you.' She leaned back. 'Can you ask God if it's "classified"?'

'What do you mean by "classified"?'

'It means that I can't give you the information. If I try to, I trigger a reaction. Unless you work out exactly what the problem is, without any input from me, then what you've done for me so far isn't enough.

And unless you discern the issue exactly and deal with it perfectly, I kill myself or I kill one of you.'

Now I have to explain about a flaw in my own personality. It's worse than a flaw; it's actually part of my sin nature. When confronted by situations like this, other people freak out and go to pieces. Not me. I am not normally parentally inverted but it's times like this when my latent got-to-be-the-parent-right-here-right-now attitude takes over.

I felt as if our prayer team had suddenly been catapulted into the movie, *The Bourne Identity*. Right into the denouement scene at the finale.

I have a plan, I thought. *It's impossible to be perfectly right, so the thing to do is be completely and utterly wrong. It won't get us anywhere but it'll be safe. The trap is sprung if we get this* partly *right.*

So, because no one in the prayer ministry team had any better idea and because I'd had a bizarre dream the previous night about a mysterious E on a ring the woman was wearing, that's what we did. Prayer on the basis that the problem was to do with the E at Delphi, but prayer that also included all the creative sidelights I'd come up with for *Balthasar's Star*. It was wild, wacky and followed no logic except a rabbit-trail of dreams and imagination.

And it wasn't perfectly wrong. It was perfectly right.

The woman said many people had handed her the same pieces of the jigsaw I gave her, but no one previously had ever put them together.

It was the moment of discovery: there are 'seals' that govern thresholds.

These seals are 'classified'; hidden; unknowable. If you take out one in prayer, the other (or others) are designed to automatically spring to life—and kill.

Seals have to be revealed by the Holy Spirit; they can only be safely opened by Jesus. He's the only bomb disposal expert who can do this. There can be up to seven seals, so you need to ask God how many of them there are. They need to be disarmed by Jesus simultaneously.

Thresholds are immensely dangerous places.

Your hand needs to be in the hand of God every step of the way.

Because threshold covenants are linked to name covenants and the satan has claimed every name. He wants both the power of birth as well as the power of rebirth. And, as you determine to see this process through to the end, for however long it takes, then you become a huge threat to his plans to possess all the names of the world.

Ungodly threshold covenants, name covenants, salt covenants, covenants with Death. Where do we begin to cut off these defiling structures in our families so we can inherit the fullness of life Jesus promises, along with a restored identity and destiny? My interpretation of Isaiah 28:15–18 is that the threshold or cornerstone covenant is the kernel, and is bonded with the name covenant. The outer layers are the covenant with Death and false refuges. We start at the outside and work inwards.

In saying 'work', I don't mean to imply this is something we accomplish ourselves. We don't 'do' it for God. We are co-workers with Him. We are dead in our sins and unable to do anything when it comes to the blood covenant but, when other covenants are involved, He wants us to be awake and part of the process.

It's still a matter of total grace on His part. But that doesn't mean it's easy.

We can think we're sitting back at rest, leaving it all up to God—when in fact we're just doing nothing. We've fallen into the hands of Rachab the Do-Nothing and are wasting time, talent and opportunity.

To begin this work of preparing for these three covenants with Jesus, we first eliminate our false refuges and our covenant with Death. I have discussed these at length in *God's Poetry*, the first book in this series. I don't believe it's wise to attempt any dismantling of a threshold covenant without dealing with these issues first. It's not only dangerous, it's highly unlikely to succeed. You can't expect your destiny and identity to be restored while the Angel of Death still has a trading agreement, signed and sealed, covering every generation in your family forever. Your inheritance may be returned to you, only to be whipped away more comprehensively than ever.

As you work on these issues, it's important to be in continual touch with the Holy Spirit. It's vital to deal with these matters in right order—and also impossible. We'll make mistakes. So we must constantly be calling on God for grace. We must not assume His grace will automatically cover every danger: that's presumption. Sometimes He'll inspire us to go in a different direction—to move out of harm's way or stop for a long time and wait patiently for the path to clear. If His Spirit prompts us to pray about a particular matter, it's because His grace is available but it is not pre-set.

Our prayer not only needs to be specific but also with permission.

Permission is something I don't fully understand—but I've experienced both sides of it. I've experienced the moment when God granted me permission to ask Him to deal with some of the dark spirits guarding territorial thresholds; when He told me what specifically to ask Him for; and that, before that time, I had authority but I didn't have permission.

Within days, I'd also experienced two balls of slurried ice slamming down onto my head. They came out of an abruptly darkened sky and brought me to a standstill just outside a place He'd prompted me about thirteen years previously. For most of those years I'd been planning to revisit to pray there. When I asked God about the iceballs, He explained I *didn't have permission*—and I wasn't going to get it.

Authority is not mandate. Jesus had the authority to ask for twelve legions of angels at his arrest, but He didn't have permission.

Those icy slaps in the face really got my attention and made me deeply conscious of ensuring I had permission from then on. But also I'm confident of this: God wants—yes, deeply desires, passionately yearns and so very utterly longs—to give us permission to ask for His overcoming power.

Providing we pass the pre-requisite tests.

Our natural inclination as human beings is to want a formula to deal with Leviathan, Python, Rachab and their minions. But God doesn't want to give us a method to pass over the threshold; He wants to give us a Guide. Himself. He wants us to pass the tests by trusting Him.

On the far side of the threshold I was astonished at how many tests I had to re-do. I suddenly discovered how many I'd failed to even recognise. One time my car broke down and I'd prayed furiously for it to be fixed. Now I realised God had wanted me to pray for the place *where* I'd broken down.

Abraham, valiant man of faith that he was, had to re-take a test he'd failed just after cutting a threshold covenant with God. He failed a second time, again choosing to identify Sarah as his sister, not his wife. This failure seems to have meant the identical test passed to the next generation: yet Isaac also failed. By the next generation, the test mutated and warped but the motif of a sister-deception in a bridal arrangement is still evident.

A test isn't a temptation to sin: rather it's a trial to find out if we'll trust God in a crisis. It's also about our willingness to re-visit our failures under the Holy Spirit's mentorship as He seeks *'to humble and test you so that in the end it might go well with you.'* (Deuteronomy 8:15–16 NIV)

Abram's first covenant with God took place just after he'd dealt with a combined gang like no other. A bunch of bandits with unpronounceable names like Chedorlaomer swooped down on the cities of the plain and made off with a massive haul of loot and captives. Amongst those taken was Abram's nephew, Lot.

Steven Collins makes an excellent case for understanding Abram, in contemporary terms, as a warlord who owed his allegiance to Melchizedek, the King of Salem.[74] Collins sees Abram as, in effect, a mercenary hired to protect Salem with his band of 318 highly trained warriors. It's possible that Lot functioned similarly at Sodom—hence why, as a foreigner, he had the privilege of sitting at the gate amongst the town council.

The lavish thanks of the King of Sodom for retrieving the booty and prisoners taken from his city may well have been a not-so-subtle bribe to lure Abram away from Salem.

This was a test. What would have happened shortly afterwards, if Abram had made a different choice? What if he'd upped and left for Sodom? Would God have then appeared to him to make a blood covenant? Would He later have said, 'I am El Shaddai, your shield and very great reward. Walk before Me and be holy,' and exchanged names in a second covenant?

I don't think so.

Abram might never have become Abraham. In choosing Sodom over Salem, he'd have chosen wealth as his reward, rather than God. In ignoring the covenant he already had with Melchizedek, he would have lost God's favour.[75]

God is a covenant-keeping God.

David, the man after God's own heart, had a dark side as an adulterer, a murderer, a liar, a manipulator, an emotionally-abusive father. As a monarch, he not only expected others to be complicit in his crimes but he also put his grief for his erring children above the national interest.

Saul, his predecessor as king, was comparatively free of David's vices. Saul's dark side was driven by jealousy and a depression directly traceable to the generational curses resulting from the near-genocide in his hometown during the era of the Judges. Yet Saul is overwhelmingly seen as a bad king and David as a good one.

What made David a 'man after God's own heart' and Saul not?

I think it's simply covenant-keeping.

David, for all his weaknesses, was a covenant-keeping man. Saul, for all his greater aspects, was not—either on a personal level, with David, or on a national level with the Gibeonites, the wood-hewers and water-carriers with whom Joshua had covenanted in a previous generation.

Abram too was a covenant-keeping man, as he demonstrated when the King of Sodom tried to bribe him.

So, for us today: Salem or Sodom? It's a choice we all have to face, sooner or later. To keep covenant or not.

Yet, even if we do so, sometimes it seems we're reaping the curses of having violated covenant instead. It's not always about us. Sometimes it's about our ancestors. It's about the curses descending from their covenant violations. Even if those covenants should never have been undertaken in the first place.

A terrible famine in the time of King David caused him to fall before God and ask why all the people's prayers were remaining unanswered.

Have you got unanswered prayers? Do things remain terribly, terribly wrong despite your tear-soaked pleas to God?

Heaven's answer to David was that his predecessor, Saul, had broken the covenant with the Gibeonites. Now that covenant should never have existed in the first place. Joshua and the Israelites, as they entered the Promised Land centuries previously, had been tricked by the Gibeonites. But that was totally irrelevant.

It's totally irrelevant whether your ancestors took out a covenant they shouldn't have. It's totally irrelevant whether they were tricked by other people or by spiritual powers. It's totally irrelevant whether or not you personally have agreed to the covenant. What have you done about renouncing it? Have you asked God to nullify it?

As the satan accuses you day and night and holds up the legal papers of covenant for your family, have you asked Jesus to take those papers from him?

If the name covenant of your family includes a dedication to an idol then, unless one of your ancestors has done something about the issue, it's still current. This is not an issue on which anyone can be complacent, even if your generational stream is stacked with godly men and women. The satan will continue to try to defile your name because he wants every last one of them as a trading token. He wants to be able to take your identity and destiny and use it as a bargaining chip.

Our names are not meant to belong to the satan through a name covenant. They are meant to be hidden, protected and nurtured within the name of God. In the modern world, names are no longer the power to summon us into our destiny. We have forfeited our inheritance to an enemy who has used them to enslave us.

So how do we get our names back?

Because of the sheer overwhelming individuality of names, every route will be slightly different. There is never a formula. The Holy Spirit will direct us all on a different, grace-filled journey.

7

Fourteen Steps

BEFORE WE CAN BECOME the radiant Bride, we need to deal with name covenants and threshold covenants. Is it coincidence that the first person to meet the Risen Christ is someone who had, a week previously, just got her name covenant back into alignment with Him? Or that the first man to go into the tomb had only recently been through a trial regarding his name covenant?[76] I don't think so.

Yet, there are some matters we should attend to before we can even think about name covenants. See the **Appendices** for suggested *prayer **guidelines*** for the following.

First:

Renew our covenant vows and baptismal promises, making sure the power structure of your words emphasises God and His grace, not ourselves. If you've asked Jesus into your life, but never asked Him to take you into the wound in His side, it's time to revisit your request for salvation. If you've asked Jesus to be your Saviour but never your Lord, it's time to ask Him for the empowerment of grace to surrender. If you've said a prayer to invite Jesus into your heart but never repented, it's time to ask Him for the power to turn away from sin. If you've never renounced the satan and all his works and all his empty promises and all the covenants over your family as well as legal agreements or occult mantles he might want to pass on to you, it's time to speak words of renunciation aloud.

Second:
Pray for God to restore your belief in a 'happy ending'. So many Christians I've encountered do not really believe that God can make a difference in their situation. When I ask them to search their hearts to see if they do believe in a 'happy ending', they admit they hope against hope but, deep down, when they are completely honest with themselves, they think God answers prayer for other people but not for them.

Third:
Pray for God to place a hedge of protection around your memory. The satan's most efficient strategy to keep you away from God is not temptation to sin but failure to remember you have sinned. Or a failure to remember, when a significant insight comes to light, what it is. Apart from the fact that it's always better to pray, gathered as 'two or three', there is a very practical side to this admonition when it comes to memory. A prayer partner is very likely to remember what you've forgotten: this is particularly true when it comes to threshold covenants. I never cease to be amazed at the people who exclaim in surprise at key revelation regarding a threshold but who have forgotten it a day later. So often a prayer partner will be stunned enough to ring me and check that what *she* remembered is correct. The spirit in charge of forgetting can also be adept at twisting. This is particularly true where shame is involved. This spirit will help us to rewrite our own personal history so we are the innocent ones in all circumstances. Such a spirit won't even let you get to the end of this paragraph before you've forgotten you intended to pray for that hedge of protection around your memory.

Fourth:
Renounce your false refuge. A false refuge is the place where you find comfort when you're disappointed or afraid. Our true refuge is God. But when we're disappointed or disillusioned with Him, we seek comfort in things. Some seem innocent while others are obviously

sinful. But, make no mistake about the ones that seem harmless, these are the hardest to eradicate. Primarily because they are so hard to recognise. Yet all of them are destructive, all are sinful.

It is best to do this with a trusted group of fellow Christians. A false refuge is associated with covenant with Death and a covenant, by its nature, is corporate in essence. So to renounce a false refuge as a private individual without the prayer and agreement of the Body of Christ defeats the entire purpose of what you are trying to achieve. This means that, if you've been avoiding other believers because you've been wounded by the Church, you need to get out of the trap of hurt that the satan has caged you in and seek help.

Fifth:

Pass the test. You will be disappointed again. You will be disillusioned. If you've truly renounced your false refuge, then you'll seek God first, not that place of comfort. You'll run to Him and ask what went wrong, why His promises have seemingly failed.

God... led you through that great and terrible wilderness, in which were fiery serpents and scorpions and thirsty land where there was no water; who brought water for you out of the flinty rock... that He might humble you and that He might test you, to do you good in the end.

Deuteronomy 8:14–16 NKJV

Look at what immediately precedes the rationale for the divine test: the mention of fiery serpents and scorpions. The serpents are symbols of Python and Rachab, and scorpions of Leviathan.

If you fail the test, simply admit it to God and ask Him for His grace to succeed and an opportunity to try again.

If you have an inordinate fear of failure, ask for His grace so that that very fear will not to draw you into the failure you dread.

And if you have an inordinate fear of success, ask for His help so that that fear will not cause you to take unconscious steps towards your comfort zone of failure.

And yes, all these matters of 'if' need to be subject to Paul's admonitions in 1 Corinthians 13 and to his encouragements in 2 Timothy 2:11–13.

Sixth:

Renounce your covenant with Death. Again, it's important to do this with at least one other trusted person. As for a false refuge, to renounce a covenant as a private individual without the prayer and agreement of the Body of Christ defeats the entire purpose of what you'd be trying to achieve.

Seventh:

Wait.

Wait. Wait.

Surprise, surprise! The seventh step is *rest*. Wait for the Lord's signal. Resting and waiting for the Lord to act is difficult in a world of instant gratification. However, this is a watchful rest. You're looking for a signal. And it's going to be something for which your camera should always be ready. It'll be awesome: an 'unnatural natural' phenomenon. Something that shouldn't happen—but does. God promises in Isaiah 28:21 that, when He breaks off a covenant with Death, He will give a 'strange' or 'alien' sign. The examples He cites are the sun standing still, or an inland tsunami. In practice, as also recorded in Scripture, He's also given a downpour of meteorites, mysterious earthquakes and a total solar eclipse when the moon was on exactly the wrong side of the earth.

From my experience in praying for people, He's also given night rainbows and 'sun dogs' in the tropics, snowflakes in summer heat, stars in the 'wrong' position and weirdly coloured skies. It's always something that takes you aback and makes you think, 'That's unusual,' just before you realise, 'That's impossible!'

How long does it take for the signal to arrive? People often ask me this. The answer: as long as it takes. Usually months.

This means you have to be committed to the process. You have to stick with God, expecting Him to answer, even when it's started to seem extremely unlikely.

Eighth:

You've attended to all the preliminaries? Now it's time to pray about your name. Once you've seen the sign that your covenant with Death is annulled, you're ready. Now it's my opinion it's not a good idea to enter into a new name covenant with Jesus at this point. The reason being that, if you go this route, you only have six days to enter into a threshold covenant as well—and that could be problematical. If you've already changed your name at some point, you're probably well aware that things don't necessarily work out the way you'd hoped. Perhaps the way is not clear for a threshold covenant—it certainly won't be if you have undealt-with sin in your life.

The covering of grace does not extend to deliberate sin, consciously indulged in, that is characterised by a refusal to repent or forgive. The interpretation of what grace is and does should never exalt what Paul wrote above what Jesus said. The human heart, cunning and crafty as it is, tries to justify a theological understanding of grace outside of Christ's parameters.

God does not wink at sin. If we are not horrified by our own sins, if we are not sick at heart that our behaviour has added to the suffering Jesus endured on the Cross, if we don't see ourselves as beggars needing God's power to enable us to love so we will cease to inflict that suffering on Jesus—and our fellow humanity—we've missed the point of grace.

After years of self-deceit, it's worth considering a course in sanctification, if for no other reason than that it will reveal the forgotten or hidden sins blocking your way forward or standing in the way of answered prayer.

When it comes to relationships between the genders, for instance, 1 Peter 3:7 tells us what hinders prayer.

When it comes to the commandments, for instance, Paul emphasises the promise for honouring our parents—and, by implication, what will happen if we don't.

We can't clear our name covenants, if we still harbour unresolved personal sin. If there's a continuation of a destructive pattern in your life—things that repeatedly drive you 'crazy'—it's time to seek spiritual counsel on their causes.

My personal recommendation is for a ministry of sanctification that is comprehensive and requires a time commitment; looks at common issues affecting us like our Perception of God, Performance Orientation, Parental Inversion, Slumbering Spirit, Captive Spirit, Inner Vows, Personal Strongholds—all the sorts of ungodly gunk that can litter our lives without our awareness. John Arnott of Toronto Airport church reportedly said that he only agreed to go for such prayer counseling because he thought it would help his wife—but, by the end of the first week, he realised he unknowingly harboured over two dozen blasphemous attitudes he needed to deal with.

There are many and varied kinds of courses available to help us grow in sanctification. Issues of shame and trauma often require outside help. Some courses are short and require just a few hours—and some involve many dozens of lessons and group ministry times. Each has their place, depending on what you need—and you should be in constant communication with God about the best one for you. The important thing is to be in community; not to try personal sanctification alone with just a book, a video or audio teaching for a guide.

Most of us want a solution to our threshold problems without having to clean up our lives. God doesn't work that way.

Most of us want to think we are ready and that the issues holding us back are mostly the fault of other people.

Get over your own innocence. The other person can be 100% at fault but that doesn't make you 100% innocent. A covenant following the blood line of your family is an agreement with the Enemy which can defile the other person.

Get over your own guilt. If God is prepared to forgive you, why do you sit in His place and pronounce what you've done as unforgiveable? If the reason is because you're so ashamed, then you need to come out of agreement with the Enemy.

Ninth:
Begin work to deal with the threefold guard of the threshold: the watch, the stone and the seals that parallel the watch, the stone and the seals placed over the tomb of Jesus.

Start here by asking God's permission if it's appropriate to petition Him for the cherubim to be placed on your own personal threshold. This is a perilous undertaking. Do not presume or make assumptions. If God's answer is 'no', go back to step 8. If the answer is 'yes', just do it. But do it, asking God also if it's wise to petition Him in line with the prayers of Kol Nidre, mentioned back on page 103.

It may be that, around this time, you sense the Holy Spirit asking you to fast—either totally or partially—as well as pray. This is in line with Scripture. Jesus' statement that 'this kind does not go out, except by prayer and fasting' (Matthew 17:21 NIV) is given immediately following a threshold covenant event: the Transfiguration.

Tenth:
Ask for any healing that may be necessary as the result of the prolonged activity of ungodly threshold guardians in your life. Such high level spirits include—but are not restricted to—Python (spirit of constriction), Rachab (spirit of wasting), Leviathan (spirit of backlash), Vampire (spirit which stakes or impales victims spiritually to the threshold), Janissary (spirit of treason which trains up young children to 'kill' their parents, either literally or figuratively). I believe that there are two other threshold spirits operating, making a total of seven in all. The last two are the spirit of Forgetting and the spirit of Rejection. These seven threshold spirits mimic the seven spirits around the throne of God.

The spirit of Rejection is by far the most difficult of all spirits to dislodge from a person's life. I've known of many people who have had wonderful ministry with a powerful sense of release from Rejection—only to have it return with a vengeance six months later.

Now it's quite likely that anyone seeking to get rid of it is going the wrong way about things. In my view, it may well be impossible to remove the legal right for a spirit of Rejection to be on the threshold.

This is the satan's last, perhaps most clever, ploy. The true threshold in anyone's life is meant to be Jesus—*the stone that the builders rejected*. Rejection is therefore inherent in the threshold. That's why the satan parks the spirit of Rejection close by, so that you'll mistake it for Jesus the Rejected One and fall into its clutches.

If it's impossible to dismiss the spirit of Rejection completely, what are we to do? I believe that the answer is the same as the one God gave to Cain when He rejected his offering and talked about sin crouching at the threshold: *rule over it.*

We are called to rule over rejection, not to dispose of it.

Eleventh:

Repent of dishonouring anyone and anything. If we have despised, slandered or cursed ourselves, our parents, other individuals, humanity as a whole, men, women, authority, government, our employee or employees, the earth itself or the creatures on it—then we have invited retaliation into our lives. This will particularly come into play after crossing the threshold, so get rid of it beforehand. Now is an acceptable time.

If we have despised the Word of God, we also need to repent. Such contempt can be subtle—we can believe the New Testament supersedes the Old. Yet the books of the 'Old Testament' are the only Scriptures Jesus used; they are the Scriptures the Bereans searched when they honorably examined what Paul preached; they are the Scriptures Paul was referring to when he told Timothy *'all Scripture is breathed out by God and profitable for teaching, for reproof, for correction, and for training in righteousness.'* (2 Timothy 3:16 ESV)

If we have gossiped or smeared another's name, we have engaged in slanderous name-trading.

If we have cursed celestial beings—including the satan, Python, Rachab, Leviathan, Vampire, Janissary or any others such as the Jezebel, Ahab or Absalom spirits—we need to repent before God. Slandering is a work of the satan. If we have indulged in the cursing of demonic spirits, principalities, powers or world rulers, we are in violation of the Scriptural injunction in Jude 1:8. All we are allowed to do is to ask God to rebuke these powers. We have to understand that, in slandering or despising any being in heaven above, earth below or even in the pit of hell, we are coming into agreement with the satan—and showing contempt for God's creation and the perfection He originally intended. We also need to understand that the gifts and calling of God are irrevocable. (Romans 11:29) The satan's high rank has not yet been stripped from him, nor has it been taken from his legion commanders.

Tom Hawkins was a counsellor specialising in helping victims of SRA (Satanic Ritual Abuse). After many years of practice, he reached an unpalatable conclusion: that although he was able to substantially help many people, the process of healing was so slow he had to admit that the fullness of life Jesus promised in John 10:10 would never become a reality for his clients in their lifetime.

Coming across the theological perspectives of Michael Heiser pertaining to the concept of the Divine Council in Scripture, he developed an appeal to the court of heaven. It uses legal language, great formality and gives careful thought to jurisprudence as outlined by Scripture. It also relies heavily on grace and guidance by the Holy Spirit. Hawkins reiterates, time and time again, the importance of honour—in particular, he emphasises the disastrous consequences of violation of Jude 1:8, the admonition not to slander celestial powers. Implicit in his outlines are calls for repenting any presumption that may have led a person to oppose such beings *without permission* in past prayers.

The template for such an appeal comes back to the Book of Job. In all of Job's arguments with God, he never dishonours Him. He ignores the satan completely and directs his appeals to God. In the end, he effectively asks for a judgment from God: he basically appeals to the Divine Council.

Twelfth:

Find out what's written on your own personal threshold stone.

Throughout Scripture, threshold stones are engraved. The words on the cornerstone mentioned in Isaiah 28:16, which both Peter and Paul quote and apply to Jesus, are *'Those who believe will not be in haste'*; also rendered, *'Those who believe will not be dismayed.'*

If you've experienced unremitting constriction, wasting or backlash, then whatever the words on your own threshold stone are, they won't be these. Nor will they be the words of Zechariah 4:7, *'Grace to it, grace to it!'* Nor will they be either of the inscriptions found in 2 Timothy 2:19, *'The Lord knows those who are His,'* or, *'Everyone who confesses the name of the Lord must turn away from wickedness.'*

How does anyone find out what's on their threshold stone?

The simplest way I've found is to complete the following statement with the very first thing that comes to mind: 'If ever I were to come into my destiny, then———'

My answer was: someone will be hurt, wounded, punished or killed.

Other people have testified to me:
- I will die.
- I will lose my loved ones.
- This is an absurd question; I can't come into my destiny.
- Other people will be injured.
- All I've worked to achieve will be destroyed.

Why would anyone enter into their destiny when, at the deepest level, they believe that any of these is the price of passing the threshold. Such beliefs are core to our being. They almost certainly exist from conception and are reinforced by the circumstances of life. They come from the very beginning of the family line.

Repent of this belief. Renounce it.

But don't do anything further about it until the end of the next step.

Thirteenth:

Ask the Holy Spirit to reveal the seals of hell. Whatever God does is counterfeited by the Enemy. Since God has sealed us as Christians in the Holy Spirit, the satan attempts to seal us for himself. This is the 'classified' information which, when revealed, is designed to spring a trap. We cannot open the seals ourselves. We cannot by logic or rational inquiry discover them.

Anyone who hopes for a formulaic process to get across the threshold is stymied at this point. All we can hope for is to recognise the number and nature of the seals through the revelation of the Holy Spirit. There can be up to seven seals and it can take many months for them all to be revealed.

Once we know what they are, we can ask Jesus to open them. He is the only one with the power to do so safely.

In my experience, seals are in some way connected to the covenant over our names. I'm not sure if this is an invariable rule but I have never yet found a case where it wasn't so. Seals always seem to be as 'strange' and 'alien' as the work of God in nullifying a covenant with death. Examples I have encountered are the letter 'e', fire and water, a pearl, a silver hand, a fox, a basket, red leaves, a pair of entwined dragons, canary yellow. Of course, these are not harmful in themselves. The spiritual power that these symbols represent can only be tackled by Jesus.

During the period of time that it takes for these seals to be revealed, additional false refuges may become apparent. Ones you've long forgotten but which need to be repented of, nevertheless. If they do, simply revisit step 4 and 5.

Once all the seals are uncovered, pray about them all at the same time, asking Jesus to open them and release the automatic traps without anyone being hurt. Be guided by the Holy Spirit in these prayers and pray over all aspects of your name that it will be completely infilled with the name of Jesus.

Again, let me emphasise that this should be prayer received

through the agency of small group of at least two or three other people. It should not be undertaken by a lone individual in private prayer. Throughout this process, covenants are the key issue, and covenants are not solitary in nature. Furthermore, it is a biblical principle to have two or three witnesses to covenantal undertakings.

Then, within six days, receive further prayer, preferably from the same group. This prayer should ask Jesus to take up your personal threshold stone—the one with the faulty inscription that you've repented of—and immediately replace it with Himself as cornerstone. Ask Him to pulverise the old threshold stone. Also ask Him to write a new inscription on your new stone.

Whenever I've prayed for this replacement stone for someone, they've felt a bit 'wobbly' for the next few days, so don't be concerned if that happens.

Wait.

About nine months. This is a birth process and the removal of the seals and restoration of name covenant is analogous to the moment of conception. The replacement of the threshold stone is analogous to the moment when new destiny settles into the womb of heaven and draws nurture from El Shaddai, the all-sufficient, strong-breasted one.

Fourteenth:

Take your first baby steps into the court of heaven by faith. You've just reached your own personal Rosh Hashanah and the court of heaven and earth is about to be called into session. The Jewish rabbis are not wrong about that. Generally speaking, we've lost sight of this truth. Your New Year has arrived and the book of your life is about to be opened and your destiny revealed.

Part of that destiny is to join the court.

Another part is to judge angels.

In fact, you'll have been in training for that role since at least step 9, if not before.

Yet another part is to negotiate with God.

Err, *what? Negotiate* with God?

Yep. I'm not kidding.

Straight after Abraham celebrated a threshold and a salt covenant with God, God confided in him about what was to happen at Sodom. And Abraham, famously, began to negotiate regarding the fate of that town.

Straight after Jesus celebrated a threshold covenant with God at the Mount of Transfiguration, He healed a boy, then sent out seventy disciples in pairs. The number is significant—He was making an earthly shadow of heaven's Divine Council: the place for negotiation with God.

When a threshold covenant is put into right order, we can get beyond pleading and even arguing with God—we can start negotiating with Him.

Now just about every commentary I've read or sermon I've heard categorically says you can't bargain with God, but that's not entirely true. Abraham is far from the only example of a person who heard God's plans and started bargaining—Jacob negotiated for a blessing while getting a new name and crossing a threshold (Genesis 32); Joshua negotiated with the Captain of the Lord's Hosts after re-affirming a covenant and crossing a threshold (Joshua 5); Amos negotiated with God about the fate of Israel (Amos 7); Ezekiel negotiated with God about the kind of dung he could use for cooking fuel (Ezekiel 4); Moses negotiated with God about His proposal to abandon the idolatrous Israelites and start over (Exodus 32); Habakkuk negotiated with God about the apparent lack of a divine answer to his complaint (Habakkuk 1); Micaiah revealed the negotiation in the courts of heaven over how Ahab would be lured to his death (1 Kings 22);[77] Mary negotiated with Jesus at the threshold event of the wedding of Cana (John 2); so did the Syro-Phoenician woman who wanted just the crumbs from the Master's table (Matthew 15).

A close examination of God's dealings with the prophets reveals that He is not an autocratic ruler. Amazingly, there's a lot of democratic wiggle-room in the courts of heaven: God consults, heeds pleas, changes His mind on the basis of prayers and appeals, subject to various conditions—see for example, His reversal of judgment on Nineveh or

His willingness to moderate the scale of punishment in Amos 7.

Who else appears in the court of heaven?

Well, for a start, the satan currently has a reserved spot there. Accusing us day and night of sin and generational iniquity, he keeps insisting on our allegiance to him—through our own mean, drab sins and, more importantly, through the ancestral covenants we've conveniently ignored because our theology tells us they can't exist.

How could we have got the kingship of God so wrong?

How could we have failed to see the consultative leadership style and pictured Him instead as a dictatorial monarch? We've imaged Him as a very benevolent, compassionate despot to be sure, but still far from democratic.

Every translator brings to the table his own biases and agenda. The Word of God is transcendent—accomplishing a perfect work of salvation through Jesus, despite the foibles and imperfections of any one version.

Our views of God's kingship have largely been formed by the most influential English translation of all time—the King James Version. At the time it was authorised, there were several other English translations available. The Geneva, the Tyndale and the Coverdale are only a few of the more well-known. None of these suited the religiously-minded James VI of Scotland when he ascended the English throne as James I of a united kingdom. And they didn't suit him because they didn't support his own personal view of the 'Divine Right of Kings'.

Paradoxically, as well as presenting an authoritarian view of God as king, it also put Him down. The most common translation of the divine title is LORD God. In a hierarchy, a king is always higher than a lord. This is an insight into what James may really have thought about the relative position of God and himself.

This is just a tiny example of the defilement that happens when we bring our own agenda into our theology. Many of us have been taught that we have direct access into the Holy of Holies—the throneroom of God—because of the veil that was torn when Jesus died.

But our experience denies our theology.

Ungodly covenants—name, threshold, blood, salt—block our access to the throneroom, the courts of heaven and the divine council.

Godly covenants—name, threshold, blood, salt—grant us access to the throneroom, the courts of heaven and the Divine Council.

Fourteen steps. To be completed—normally—over a period of about fourteen months. Probably it seems too much. Too intensive. Too hard. Too programmed. Too legalistic. Too pressured. In a word: impossible.

There is another way.

Put your hand in the hand of Jesus, and let Him walk you through and talk you through. I didn't have this plan when I started out with several near-strangers who agreed to pray together about their names. When I felt God was suggesting to me to ask for the cherubim to be placed on our thresholds, it seemed crazy at first. Only later when we discovered the presence of Python and Rachab—and their counterfeiting operation—did His suggestion make sense.

Every step of this process has been a footfall into semi-darkness for us. Some moments have been frightening. Those moments when we've realised just how mighty and terrifying and unbelievably powerful certain spirits of the threshold really are. Ultimately, however, it's only led to a much greater appreciation of who God is. Not just how majestic He is, but also how magisterial.

We've had to throw away all our pre-conceptions of Him and look at what the Bible *really* says.

If we can make it across this threshold, you can too.

Because it's not the mightiness of our faith or the power of our prayers that has brought us here. Our faith is a handful of mustard seeds at best; our prayers—well, mine seem to be getting more pathetic as time goes on. There are days when they resonate with power, beauty and persuasion but that, I realise, is God's grace to encourage the faith of others. When I'm by myself, I'm conscious of their triviality and inadequacy. I keep having to thank God that it's not my words that make a difference, but Jesus as the One who mediates and empowers my prayers. And I keep having to thank Him that the Holy Spirit graces us with fruit and gifts to enable us to stand up to foes that make Goliath look like a grasshopper.

A good day to start your journey towards the court of heaven is today.

Just lift your face for the kiss of God and, through that kiss, receive His armour. Then put your hand in His and take the first step towards your true calling.

Appendix 1 — Renewal of Baptismal Vows

I ask you now to renew your baptismal promises:
Do you renounce Satan?
I do.
And all his works?
I do.
And all his empty promises?
I do.
And every covenant, pledge, vow and agreement that binds you into oneness with him or his servants?
I do.
Do you turn away from the allurements of evil, so that sin may have no mastery over you?
I do.
Do you repent of your sin, so as to live in the freedom of the children of God?
I do.
Do you believe in God, the Father Almighty, Creator of heaven and earth?
I do.
Do you believe in Jesus Christ, his only Son, our Lord, who was born of the Virgin Mary, lived in Nazareth, suffered death and was buried in Jerusalem, rose again from the dead and is seated at the right hand of the Father?
I do.
Do you believe in the Holy Spirit, the true and holy and universal church known to God, the communion of saints, the forgiveness of sins, the resurrection of the body, and life everlasting?
I do.
Do you answer Jesus' invitation to be born of water and the spirit and become His bride?
I do.
Do you, even now, enter His wounds by grace through faith?
I do.
So, may almighty God, the Father of our Lord Jesus Christ, who has given us new birth by water and the Holy Spirit and brought us into His covenant and offered us forgiveness of our sins, keep us by his grace, in Christ Jesus our Lord, for eternal life. Amen.

Appendix 2 — Prayer for Belief in a Happy Ending

This prayer, like all those in these appendices, should be used as a guideline, not as a formula.

Heavenly Father, I confess that, hidden in the deepest part of my heart, I've tucked away a thought that I find it so hard to admit. I don't really believe that You have plans and a future for me that include a happy ending. I don't really think You're going to give me a fairytale finale to the story of my life. Maybe the poem You're making out of other people's names will be full of wonder, but I suspect mine will either wind up in outright tragedy or just simply frustration and desperation. When it comes right down to it, I guess I have doubts about the greatest happily-ever-after ending of all: the resurrection of Jesus. My head and my heart are disconnected. I don't think I can really participate in His fullness of resurrection life.

Father, forgive me. I ask that, by Your mercy, You slay this attitude of faithlessness in me and nail it to the cross of Your son, Jesus of Nazareth. I ask that, by Your mercy, You resurrect in me a firm and holy belief that the prophetic words of Jeremiah 29:11 NIV are true for me and my loved ones: '*I know the plans I have for you, plans to prosper you and not harm you, plans to give you hope and a future.*'

Father, thank You for this promise. May You be glorified in my happy ending.

In the name of Jesus of Nazareth. Amen.

Appendix 3 — Prayer for Protection of Memory

This prayer, like all those in these appendices, should be used as a guideline, not as a formula.

Father God, I ask You to put Your own guard on my memory and especially my amygdala, the repository of fear memory in my brain. I also ask You to dismiss any guard in either place not sent by You.

Please help me to remember from now on and also to seal those new memories by the power of Your Holy Spirit. Where You have sent me dreams that I have not remembered, please bring them to mind through repetition or through a series of prompts in my daily life; in either case, do not allow me to forget them again before I am able to write them down in detail.

Please also cause me to recall anything from the past that You desire me to deal with and also remind me to seek the immediate help of Your Son, Jesus Christ.

Help me also to remember to pray regularly about the restoration of my memory. I ask all these things in the name of my covenant redeemer, Jesus of Nazareth, who died for me. Amen.

Appendix 4 — Prayer to Put on the Armour of God

This prayer, like all those in these appendices, should be used as a guideline, not as a formula.

Dear God in heaven, please kiss me now. Thank You, Father! Thank You, Jesus! Thank You, Holy Spirit!

Appendix 5 — False Refuge Checklist

What activities do you use to distract yourself from disappointment? Where are the mental 'places' that you run to when you are in need of comfort or protection? What reactions make you feel better or more in control when things don't go the way you anticipated? How do you 'lick your wounds'?

In other words: how and where do you hide out from God when you are disappointed with Him?

The following list is by no means exhaustive but exemplifies the wide variety of common comforts that people use to make themselves feel better while avoiding taking refuge in God.

THOUGHTS/STRONGHOLDS

- ☐ Fantasies that arouse or comfort
- ☐ Rationalisation
- ☐ Mentally rewriting personal history
- ☐ Criticism
- ☐ Judgments
- ☐ Resentments
- ☐ Self-defence
- ☐ Blame-shifting
- ☐ Confusion
- ☐ Indecision
- ☐ Victim mentality
- ☐ Entitlement
- ☐ Self-pity
- ☐ Learned helplessness
- ☐ Comparison

ABUSE TO OTHERS

- ☐ Verbal (words spoken against others)
- ☐ Physical
- ☐ Emotional (manipulation)
- ☐ Sexual (lust, even with spouse)
- ☐ Spiritual (religious or occult control)

SUBSTANCE ADDICTION
- ☐ Food
- ☐ Gourmet treats
- ☐ Chocolate
- ☐ Coffee
- ☐ Cigarettes
- ☐ Alcohol
- ☐ Illegal drugs
- ☐ Prescription drugs
- ☐ Adrenaline

EMOTIONAL
- ☐ Anger
- ☐ Cynicism
- ☐ Indifference
- ☐ Apathy
- ☐ Helplessness
- ☐ Remorse
- ☐ Suppression / stuffing emotions
- ☐ Pride / arrogance
- ☐ Discouragement

SEXUAL ADDICTION
- ☐ Adultery (spiritual & physical)
- ☐ Pornography
- ☐ Masturbation
- ☐ Sexual fantasy
- ☐ Homosexuality
- ☐ Sexual defilement of spouse (manipulation)
- ☐ Sexual abuse of children

SELF-ABUSE or SELF-PUNISHMENT
- ☐ Verbal (thoughts / words spoken against self)
- ☐ Physical (not caring for or hurting self)
- ☐ Anorexia / bulimia

- ☐ Emotional (stuck in negative emotions)
- ☐ Spiritual (participating in the occult)
- ☐ Sexual (allowing self to be defiled)

BEHAVIOUR
- ☐ Need to be right (insecurity)
- ☐ Niceness
- ☐ Reading (books, magazines, newspaper)
- ☐ Pretence ("All is well!")
- ☐ Withdrawal
- ☐ Isolation
- ☐ Passivity
- ☐ Passive aggression
- ☐ Control / manipulation
- ☐ Blaming
- ☐ Complaining
- ☐ Thumb-sucking / nail-biting
- ☐ Overly responsible / caretaker / enabler
- ☐ The Noble Martyr (manipulation through guilt)
- ☐ Cross-dressing
- ☐ Holidays
- ☐ Beauty or hair treatments

ACTIVITY ADDICTION
- ☐ Television
- ☐ Video games
- ☐ Violent movies
- ☐ Comedy shows
- ☐ Computer / internet
- ☐ Workaholism
- ☐ Busyness
- ☐ Gardening
- ☐ Shopping
- ☐ Exercise

- ☐ Massage
- ☐ Dancing
- ☐ Emotional experiences / Emotional 'treats'
- ☐ Gambling / lottery
- ☐ Church activities / Christian conferences
- ☐ Cleaning
- ☐ Extreme sports
- ☐ Driving / racing
- ☐ Going to the doctor / counsellor / therapist

MAGIC / OCCULT
- ☐ Horoscopes / tea leaf reading
- ☐ Redecorating to enhance luck
- ☐ Fortune teller
- ☐ Séances
- ☐ Twirling (spinning on the spot)
- ☐ Wishcraft (concentration on a wish / desire)
- ☐ Wishing well / Wishing tree
- ☐ Visualisation
- ☐ Naming and claiming
- ☐ Yoga (yoked to a serpent spirit)
- ☐ Martial arts (movement dedicated to gods)
- ☐ Invoking a word, spell or incantation
- ☐ Occult books
- ☐ Ritual activity
- ☐ Asking others for prayer because their faith is greater than yours (magical thinking)
- ☐ Repetition of words / names (including prayer/ Scripture verse) to build power (magical thinking)

Copyright © 1989, 1997 Revised 2014 Elijah House, Inc., Coeur d' Alene, Idaho USA. All rights reserved. Adapted & used by permission Elijah House Ministries Australia.

Appendix 6 — Prayer to Remove the Compulsion for Haste

This prayer, like all those in these appendices, should be used as a guideline, not as a formula.

Heavenly Father, I want this mess over and done with *now*—today. I'm tired of waiting for the constriction to end. I'm fed up with the delay over Your promises to me reaching fulfilment. It's taking so long for all that's been wasted to be restored. Hope deferred has made my heart sick. My faith is a frayed rope, near breaking point.

I can hardly bear the thought that this might go on for a while yet, and that nothing I can do will speed the process. I feel undone at the prospect that Your natural timing for me in this situation might be like planting a seed before winter and waiting for it to sprout in the springtime.

Father, Your word says that inscribed my threshold should be: '*Those who believe will not be in haste*' and '*Those who believe will not be dismayed.*'

But I confess to dismay, disappointment, dread and a desire to do something—*anything*—to resolve this situation faster. I surrender to You my compulsion for haste. I ask it be nailed to the cross of Your Son, Jesus of Nazareth, and covered by His blood. I ask also that my dismay, disappointment and dread also be nailed there and covered by His blood.

When I am tempted to take back or forget this request, please remind me You make available to me the grace and power to rest in You and to wait for Your timing.

I make this prayer in the Name of Jesus of Nazareth, my covenant defender. Amen.

Appendix 7 — Renouncing a Covenant with Death

This prayer, like all those in these appendices, should be used as a guideline, not as a formula. All the prayers in these appendices are more appropriate for a small group or corporate body, rather than private individuals. This is even more especially true for this prayer, both because of the nature of covenant and because of the Biblical principle of witnesses.

The name of the Lord is a strong tower; the righteous run to it and are safe.

Proverbs 18:10 NIV

Father, on the night before Your Son died on the cross at Calvary, He made provision for a new covenant in His blood. He gave me the opportunity to come into covenant with Him, to be part of Your family, to exchange my rags of destiny for the one You intended for me when You gave me my name.

I acknowledge that I have another covenant; a covenant that is a perversion of all that You intended a covenant to be.

I recognise that I have been faithless by retaining a covenant with death that I have never renounced. Before these witnesses, I renounce my covenant with death and repent of believing the lies associated with it.

I ask for Your forgiveness for using the covenant as a refuge against fear of death and for keeping any vows that powered the covenant. I specifically renounce the deep belief of my heart that I will never come into my destiny.

Unite my heart to fear and reverence Your name.

I surrender my identity to You. I ask You to cut away from me and from my family every aspect of this covenant which dishonours You. I ask You to cut a new covenant with me, to bind me to Yourself through Your blood, to bring me into Your family and to take care of my loved ones as You would Your own.

Lord, I have nothing to give You in exchange for a new destiny. The destiny I might have given You has been robbed from me as a result of the covenant with death. I can only ask that when You nullify my covenant with death, You take back what would have been mine for Yourself. It is Yours. I make no claim on it.

Restore to me, Lord, in Your time and timing, the mantle of destiny which You have always wanted me to wear. I acknowledge that I am Your workmanship, Your poem, created in You for good works, which You prepared beforehand for me to walk in as I journey through life. Lord Jesus, Father God, Holy Spirit, walk with me. I cannot be 'me' without You.

I humbly ask You to give—and confirm—a Scripture verse for me to be cut as part of the covenant I now ratify with You.

Make us one.

In the name of the Name above all Names—Jesus of Nazareth, my Kinsman-Redeemer, the One who gave His life for me. Amen.

Appendix 8 — Prayer for Purification of a Name

This prayer, like all those in these appendices, should be used as a guideline, not as a formula.

Father in heaven, I would like to cut a name covenant with You but I await Your direction and timing for it.

In the meantime, please come as the refiner and place my name in your crucible of purification. Gently apply the fire of Your Holy Spirit to my name so all impurity is bubbled out. As each defilement over my name rises to the surface, please skim it off. Father, please work over my name seven times, as You would a crucible of silver, until such time as You can see Your own face reflected in it.

May Your crucible hold each part of my name, each letter, each syllable, each arrangement of letters and syllables, every elision between words, every nickname, workcode, pen-name, pet-name, name before birth or name before marriage.

Father, I give my name into Your keeping. If any spirit claims ownership of it, please deny that claim in Your court. If my heart is in hidden dispute with You about my name, please remind it of Ephesians 3:15–16, that You are *'the Father, from whom every family in heaven and on earth is named.'*

When You are ready, please return to me dominion of the gift You gave to Adam—that of naming—and cut a name covenant with me.

I ask this in the name of Him who is the Name above all names, Jesus of Nazareth. **Amen.**

Appendix 9 — Prayer regarding Cherubim

This prayer, like all those in these appendices, should be used as a guideline, not as a formula.

STOP! Do you have permission to pray this prayer or one like it? Ask God before you proceed. Expect His answer: after all, His sheep hear His voice.

STOP! Ask God if you should petition Him in line with the prayers of Kol Nidre on page 103.

STOP! Have you made a list of entities (terrestrial or celestial, individual or corporate, government or private) you have dishonoured and repented of defiling them? How have you actioned such repentance—mental assent is not enough. Ask the Father that, through the cross of Jesus, you NOT reap the dishonour you have sown and be cleansed of any defiling influences currently operating in your life or that you are due to reap.

Father, thank You for Your permission. I ask Your mercy regarding this request. The cherubim slay anyone who is not holy, not covered by the blood of sacrifice. There are almost certainly hidden covenants in my life that pollute the threshold, defiling it, making me as one who tramples on the blood of Jesus. I don't want to do that. I want to honour Him and You.

But I'm in a trap the Enemy has carefully planned so I can never get over this threshold. Please have mercy on me and be my covenant defender, despite those hidden covenants. As soon as I know what they are, I will renounce them. Don't turn away from me, O God. Don't pass me by—instead, be my Passover.

Please place the cherubim on all the thresholds of my life, so they can make life uncomfortable for Python and Rachab and chase them off this place I want to dedicate to You. I know You call all times 'soon', so I realise this is not an 'instant' solution. I thank You for Your mercy.

In the name of Jesus of Nazareth. Amen.

Endnotes

1. If you are puzzled that 'shem' doesn't look like 'shim' or 'sham', please remember that classical Hebrew has no vowels, however English translations include vowels to help us say the words. The vowel system created by Jewish scholars for the pronunciation of Hebrew was only formulated about a thousand years ago. It did not exist in ancient times.
2. Adam's name is a pun on *red* and *ground*. But not on *earth*, 'eretz.'
3. http://www.torah.org/features/par-kids/names.html
4. 'In the ancient world, a name was a person's identity. It was far more than a distinguishing label or an indicator of family heritage. A person's name said something about who the person was in character or nature. Most babies in Bible times were not named until the eighth day after their birth... In addition, it was a custom in Bible times that mothers spent hours singing and talking to their unborn children, bonding with them in a deep emotional and spiritual way. This bonding gave mothers special insight into the personalities and destinies of the babies in their wombs.' Michael Youssef, *Discover the Power of One: make your life count*
5. Moreover, 'ng' is often pronounced 'm' in modern Chinese, making the first syllable effectively identical with 'shem', the Hebrew word for *name*.
6. I am aware that most rabbinic commentaries, and therefore many Christian ones following that lead, specify the time period as three days. The exact number is not cited in Scripture. I have not found any commentary that cites the time period as six days. However I believe the case I have made for the parallel between what happens between Abraham and God at Hebron and what happens between Jesus and Peter at Caesarea Philippi is sufficient to indicate it was six days, not three. (See *God's Pageantry: The Threshold Guardians and the Covenant Defender*.) In addition, chapter 5 of this current book offers further evidence that the natural time period between name and threshold covenants was set at six days from the very beginning of creation.
7. See article at http://www.jesus-resurrection.info/difference-between-guilt-and-shame.html by Paul Harnett. In our culture and in our century, shame has undergone a radical shift. The function of shame is to draw our attention to guilt—and guilt, in its turn, to sin. Shame however has been taken away from sexuality, lying, cheating, dishonesty and theft. By removing the symptom, our society hopes to remove the cause: our sense of sin. But shame is part of the human condition. We can't get rid of it with its blushes and flushes and fiery sense of having stepped out of line. Harnett points out that another name for the 'asham/guilt' offering was the 'trespass' offering and that the purpose for this offering was to reveal a need in our life and to provide the means to temporarily atone for a trespass or transgression. Furthermore it was to cleanse our conscience in order to restore us to right relationship with Him.
8. Paul Harnett (see previous endnote) looks at the word differently. He sees the root as 'aysh', *fire*. He views the final letter 'mem' as *chaos* or *turbulence rising*. 'When

someone is ashamed,' he says, 'they feel flushed, as if they are "burning up". In fact, it is the consciousness of guilt they feel at that moment as the blood rises in the face. This is a certain giveaway, as understood in the expression "shame-faced." One who is ashamed, is experiencing the *fire of chaos* within.' He goes on to say that 'To be shamed by another' is a different matter. Likewise is the notion of 'perceived shame, which is rooted in fear. It is a projection of fear within.'

9   'Author and psychiatrist James Gilligan writes that the self cannot survive without love, and the self, starved of love, dies. The absence of self-love is shame, "just as cold is the absence of warmth."'' Gregory Boyle, *Tattoos on the Heart: The Power of Boundless Compassion*

10   Probably from 'qatsah' or from 'gazaz', *shear, mow, cut off, be destroyed.*

11   At the time of writing, the reconstruction of the terracotta army has now stopped for many years. It is possible to rebuild the figures. However, the halt on the reconstruction is due to the realisation that there appears to be no way of preserving the original paint. When the fragments are picked up from the earth, they lose their colour in a matter of minutes. Until such time as technology improves, allowing these hues to be preserved, it has been decided to leave them where they are.

12   Yechiel Eckstein, Holy Land Moments Daily Devotional, *May Your Will Be Done*, 12 June 2015

13   Confirming John the apostle as the identity of the writer.

14   '*Simon Peter, Thomas (called Didymus), Nathanael from Cana in Galilee, the sons of Zebedee, and two other disciples were together.*' (John 21:2 NIV) In the opening chapter, five disciples are mentioned: Andrew, Simon Peter, Philip, Nathanael and one other unnamed disciple. (John 1:40–51) In all of Scripture, Nathanael is mentioned only in these two places.

15   (1) 496 syllables at the opening and 496 words in the final scene.

(2) 17 words in the first sentence and the 17th triangular number (153) mentioned in the final scene. This is in defiance of the Greek ideal of beauty in art and literature which considered 17 to be the 'antiphraxis', variously translated as *disjunction, precaution, obstruction, barrier* and *abomination*.

(3) At the beginning there is the testimony of a man named John while, mirroring it at the end, is the testimony of the disciple Jesus loved—John the apostle.

(4) John the Baptist's testimony is about the Lamb of God, while John the apostle's final testimony is of an incident involving himself, Simon Peter and a matter of Lambs and Sheep.

(5) The five disciples listed at the beginning include Simon Peter and Nathanael and the seven disciples at the end are grouped to make five sets, which also include Simon Peter and Nathanael. As mentioned in the previous footnote, these are the only times Nathanael is mentioned anywhere in Scripture.

(6) The five disciples at the beginning follow Jesus to Galilee at the beginning of His ministry; the five sets of disciples follow Jesus to Galilee at His instruction, after the Resurrection.

(7) At the beginning, the doubts of a disciple are mentioned; likewise at the end. The disciple at the beginning is Nathanael and the one at the end is

Thomas. This is the only occasion in the ring-structure where the names do not appear to match immediately. However, it should be mentioned that the various lists of disciples in other places (Matthew 10:3; Mark 3:18; Luke 6:14; Acts 1:13) do not mention Nathanael. Tradition therefore equates him with Bartholomew, *son of Ptolemy* or *son of Talmai*. In *God's Pageantry*, I have made a case for Thomas being derived from *Talmai* or from *Ptolemy*. So if Nathanael is indeed Bartholomew and if my surmise about the derivation of Thomas is correct, then the names do indeed match, though not on the surface. It seems that John is suggesting to his readers that they should dig deeper to identify 'Nathanael' and indirectly offering a hint through the name Thomas.

(8) A woman named Mary is mentioned at the beginning and at the end. In both instances, there are bridal overtones to the event.

(9) The emptying of the Temple by Jesus is paralleled by the emptying of the tomb.

(10) Nicodemus is mentioned at the beginning and also at the end; both occasions refer to the new birth.

(11) Both at the start and the finish, there is the testimony of a man named John. At the beginning John the Baptist testifies to the Bridegroom. At the end, John the apostle testifies to Jesus' last word: 'kalah', *it is finished*, or 'kallah', *my bride*.

16 Anne Hamilton, *The Winging Word* (page 8–9), referring to the insight of CS Lewis in *Miracles* that Jesus performed miraculous signs that, in many cases, mirrored the activity of the Father in the natural world. God, for instance, turns water into wine every day in the transmutative growth of a grape-vine. He also multiplies bread when a single sown seed becomes a many-fold harvest.

17 *God's Panoply* explores the differences in the Hebrew and Greek concepts of *submission*. In some ways very similar, in other ways diametrically opposed, the distinction between them is important for understanding the Hebrew poetry behind Paul's admonitions in these instances. Without a true understanding of the mutuality of covenant and armour-bearing, it is impossible to recognise the natural train of thought from *submission* to *marriage* to *armour* in both Romans and Ephesians. All of these words go back to one of the most beautiful names of God in Scripture: Yahweh Nissi, *the Lord my banner, the God who lifts up*.

18 Brian Simmons, *John—Eternal Love*, The Passion Translation.

19 Brian Simmons on Facebook, 2 April 2015.

20 David Malcolm Bennett, *The Sinner's Prayer: Its Origins and Dangers*, Even Before Publishing 2011.

21 Kenneth Leech, *We Preach Christ Crucified*, Darton,Longman & Todd Ltd 2006.

22 In the course of writing this book I was also asked to write a short article about the Cadbury family (of Cadbury chocolate fame) and their faith. In it, I mentioned that they were devout Quakers and therefore pacifists who, when it came to World War I and II, looked for ways other than fighting to serve in the theatre of battle—such as ambulance services. As it went through the hands of several editors, these few sentences were the only ones to cause problems. Initially one editor simply wanted to delete them. I pointed out that this was an intrinsic part of the faith of the Cadburys and that it would not only be misrepresenting them but passively promoting our already-existing

violent mindset. Eventually, because I fought so hard to keep it, the sentences were kept but only in a greatly diluted form. Opposition to pacifism is so strong that it reveals the real depth of insecurity in our hearts. Like any other belief, those who are truly secure in their warrior mindset are able to consider the arguments against it without becoming aggressive in response.

23 www.fivedoves.com/letters/oct2011/rauld108.htm, accessed 30 June 2015.
24 Mark 14:1–11.
25 Luke 7:36–50.
26 John 12:1–11.
27 Simon gave Jesus the name, 'Messiah', and Jesus then gave him the name, Cephas. This Hebrew name has similar overtones to the Greek name Peter but it is not identical in meaning. As noted in *God's Poetry* and *God's Pageantry*, Peter is not simply *rock*, but has the sense of *a rock from which an enterprise is started*. Cephas is a very special rock: it's related to the threshold stone or cornerstone at the entrance to a house. It was a place of threshold sacrifice.
28 As in the case of Esther with myrrh. This raises some interesting issues, since Esther's Jewish name was Hadassah, meaning *myrtle*. The Greek word, 'mura', means both *myrrh* and *myrtle*.
29 Andrew Reid, *Exodus: Saved for Service*, Reading the Bible Today series, Aquila Press Sydney 2013. Reid goes on to say: '…on a significant number of occasions [throughout Scripture], the background to their godly action is the failure of male leadership or the absence of God-fearing men.'
30 Yechiel Eckstein, 'By the Light of the Moon', *Holy Land Moments Daily Devotional*, 19 February 2014. Eckstein goes on to explain that the women were rewarded for this attitude with a monthly holiday. Every new moon there is a mini-holiday exclusively for the women.
31 Yechiel Eckstein, 'Every End is a New Beginning', *Holy Land Moments Daily Devotional*, 25 May 2015
32 English translations just use 'say' without any differentiation.
33 And when it comes to blessing, this connection between Jacob and his grandmother might account for one of the most mysterious titles in all Scripture: the House of Jacob.
Then Moses went up to God, and the Lord called to him from the mountain and said, 'This is what you are to say to the house of Jacob and … tell the people of Israel: "You yourselves have seen what I did to Egypt … Now if you obey Me fully and keep My covenant, then … you will be My treasured possession … "'

Exodus 19:3–6 NIV

According to some rabbis, the House of Jacob in this passage is not synonymous with the people of Israel. It's not the usual poetic parallelism. They identify the House of Jacob as specifically referring to 'the women of the tribes of Israel' and suggest the text indicates that, at Mount Sinai, the women stepped forward first to accept the covenant of the Law. The Israelite men, still smarting over the golden calf, were slow to follow that lead.
34 Yechiel Eckstein, 'Passing the Tests of Faith', *Holy Land Moments Daily Devotional*, 7 July 2015

35	Gordon Dalbey, *Fight Like a Man: Redeeming Manhood for Kingdom Warfare*, Tyndale House Publishers 1995
36	See either *God's Poetry* (page 110) or *God's Panoply* (page 124).
37	It had appeared several times in the Latin Vulgate, translated by Jerome in the fourth century, but not as a name. Rather it was a generic descriptor of a shining thing like a star. http://www.crivoice.org/lucifer.html (accessed 10 September 2015)
38	http://www.babycentre.co.uk/a568884/baby-naming-practices-from-around-the-world#ixzz3bCuehZuH (accessed 10 September 2015)
39	http://www.cracked.com/article_20024_5-creepy-coincidences-you-wont-believe-actually-happened.html (accessed 10 September 2015)
40	William Schnoebelen, in *Romancing Death: A True Story of Vampirism, Death, the Occult, and Deliverance*, notes that the names of the three angels—Sanoy, Sansenoy and Samegalef—correspond to the names of the angels sent in pursuit of Lilith when she left Adam. In the legend, Lilith was Adam's first wife, created from the dust, just as he was. Proud and wilful, she abandoned Eden and, when three angels were sent after her, she refused to return, adding that in revenge she would kill toddlers, babies and infants. However where an amulet is placed, she would leave that house alone. (An obvious counterfeit and reversal of threshold covenant rites.) Ever since, her hatred of mankind has led her to roam the world looking for children to slay. Schnoebelen describes Pharisaical Judaism as a rather creepy world of talismans, incantations and superstitions which saw Lilith as a patroness of Sudden Infant Death Syndrome. He also describes Lilith, with her claw-like hands, as the origin of the vampire myth. And, while it is a myth, he points out that that doesn't mean it isn't real. Many times in his book he describes the occult term 'egregore', a thought form which, if enough people feed it by worshipping or fearing it, acquires a dynamic of its own. A demon can use this to advantage and come to empower the thought form and inhabit it.
41	One of the most famous and revered Hebrew scholars of all time, Rabbi Solomon Yitzchaki (A.D. 1040-1105) of France is said to have drawn attention to the fact—in his eleventh century *Rashi Commentary*—'that with different vowel points the original Hebrew word we now think of as meaning *heaven* ["shamayim"] would mean *fire in waters*.' (Dr. Walt Brown in *In The Beginning: Compelling Evidence for Creation and the Flood*, Center for Scientific Creation: Phoenix, AZ; 2008, 8th ed., "Something to Think About: 'Fire in Waters'." p. 374) See also Endnote 1 about vowels.
42	Possibly better rendered as the *sea of name*. Although 'names' is not strictly correct, the very sense of a sea suggests the Torah itself. Written as one long sequence of letters, without spaces—it essentially forms one vast word. Within it, the individual words of the Hebrew Scriptures can be detected. Based on this similarity, I have chosen to translate 'shamayim' as *sea of names*, rather than *sea of name*.
43	blog.beliefnet.com/fromthemasters/2011/10/our-words-create-our-worlds. html#comment-550

44 David Patterson, *Hebrew Language and Jewish Thought*, Routledge 2004

45 www.tnnonline.net/faq/A/Alef_Tav_Yeshua_as_the.pdf, accessed 28 February 2015

46 Such hospitality rites still exist: 'The hostile environment in regions such as the Sinai gave the impetus to a fabulous hospitality towards desert travellers. A complete stranger could stay with a clan for three days without being asked his intentions. He was considered and treated as a guest and enjoyed full protection. In the vast silence and brooding solitude of the Sinai, simply encountering another person was (and, in some regions, still is) an unusual and noteworthy event. A new face is cause for great interest, generosity and careful etiquette, all values celebrated in Bedouin poetry, sayings and songs. Hospitality is extensively ritualised. Whenever an animal is slaughtered for a guest, men ritually sacrifice it in accordance with Islamic law. Guests are ritually incorporated into their hosts' households because, in case of armed conflict, guests must be protected as if they were family members. When guests arrive, they are welcomed and a rug is immediately spread out and they will first be served sweet tea in small glasses. Once the guests are honoured, respected and nourished, it is time for the main ritual: the preparation of fresh cardamom-spiced Arabic coffee.
(*Bedouin Hospitality* at http://www.bedawi.com/Hospitality_EN.html) accessed 10 September 2015

47 'Ebru' or 'Hebrew' means *one who crossed over from the River*, according to Chuck Missler. Missler suggests that 'Hebron' means *communion*; this only reinforces the covenantal aspect since communion (com, *with* + union) has the sense of bringing together into oneness.

48 You may wonder which side I take in this debate. The answer is: both. As far as I am concerned, Scripture both implicitly and explicitly teaches relativity. It explicitly does so when Peter wrote, quoting Psalm 90:4 and adding some additional information: '...*with the Lord one day is as a thousand years, and a thousand years as one day*.' (2 Peter 3:8 ESV) This vastly simplifies the calculation necessary: we don't even need to know the relativistic equations to work out the time distortion. We're given it.
Relativity is implicit in Scripture in the word for *day*, 'yam'. Directly connected to the sea with its idea of deep, of currents, waves, ebbing and flowing, it implies that sometimes there might be faster movement than at others. To presume the meaning of 'yam' in one place has exactly the same meaning in another (when the very nature of the word indicates time is shifting) is to impose Newtonian rather than Einsteinian thinking on a Hebrew concept. Especially given the explicit statement from Peter.
And speaking of that explicit statement, there are, I know, several possible ways to interpret it. My own interpretation may not be correct but I remain astounded by its implications—simply take what Peter says and do the multiplication of the number of 12 hour periods (since his word could simply refer to daylight hours) in 6000 years as the supposed age of the earth. Convert the answer back into years and what is the result? 4.4 billion years as an

alternative answer.

On the one hand, there's the plain vanilla, non-relativistic, Scriptural age of the earth and on the other, there's the age ubiquitously quoted by scientists.

Sure there are questions to answer and mysteries that this raises. But, to me, it also says that neither answer is as cut and dried as it appears. We should start exploring the mystery of the divergence of God's frame of reference (to use a relativistic term) from man's frame of reference, not keep insisting that science and faith have different answers. I certainly don't, as a result, believe in evolution.

49   Looking from a different direction: if an alien located 60–65 million light years away, say in the Virgo cluster, looked in the right direction with an immensely high-resolution telescope today, it would still be able to observe dinosaurs roaming the earth.
50   It isn't possible; because of side effects due to mass.
51   This leads to Einstein's famous twin paradox.
52   By normal reckoning. Note how significant it is to specify this now. This is from Job 38:4;7.
53   Poincaré said this to contrast with the quotation: *Poetry is the art of giving different names to the same thing.*
54   Yes, logical does come from 'logos', too. It retains the sense of 'logos' as *rational mind*. Logic on the other hand retains both the rational and mathematical senses, while logarithm derives from the purely mathematical sense. Apology, theology, prologue, epilogue and suchlike lean towards the sense of 'logos' as *word*.
55   See *God's Panoply*, chapter 6, for further details. Each letter in Hebrew has a mathematical value. The gematria of each word is found by totalling the mathematical value of each letter.
     The first word in Scripture is *bereshit* and its gematria is 913.
     The second word is *bara* and its gematria is 203.
     The third word is *Elokim* (modern Hebrew spelling) and its gematria is 86.
     The fourth word is *et* and its gematria is 401.
     The fifth word is *hashamayim* and its gematria is 395.
     The sixth word is *v'et* and its gematria is 407.
     The seventh word is *haarets* and its gematria is 296.
     The first and third words add to 999, a multiple of 111.
     The second, fourth and fifth words also add to 999.
     The third, fifth and sixth words add to 888, also a multiple of 111.
     111 is used throughout medieval literature as a symbol of covenant (see *Gawain and the Four Daughters of God: the testimony of mathematics in Cotton Nero A.x*) where it appears to have been sourced in the seventeenth chapter of John's gospel, the preeminent discussion of oneness in all Scripture. The design of this chapter is based on 111. (See Maarten JJ Menken, *Numerical Literary Techniques in John: The Fourth Evangelist's Use of Numbers of Words and Syllables*, Novum Testamentum , Supplement 55, Brill Academic Publishers 1997.)

56   'Perets' is the Hebrew word for *breaking forth, breaking out, a breach, an opening, a rift, rupture* or *penetration*. First found in the Bible in Genesis 38:29, it describes the unusual birth of Perez. 'Sherets' is the Hebrew word for *swarming* or *stinging creatures*. 'Ratsa" is the word for *pierce*; while not the same lettering the rhymes above, it is a close sound.

57   See *God's Panoply* or *Gawain and the Four Daughters of God: the testimony of mathematics in Cotton Nero A.x* for my explanation of why 777, 7777, 77777 and so on are a mathematical metaphor for both the Armour of God and for a kiss.

58   From 'On Poetry', in his *Quite Early One Morning* (New York: New Directions, 1954)

59   Had his mathematical link between the armour of God and the kiss of heaven not been so strong, I would not have discovered that in Hebrew *to kiss* means *to put on armour*.

60   From Dwight Pryor's article, *Jesus—The Fullness of Tanakh*, in *Roots and Branches: Explorations in the Jewish Context of the Christian Faith*, John Fieldsend (ed.) Pryor discusses the Transfiguration at some length, pointing out that the language used during that momentous event is that of a midwife. He further points out that, just a few days prior to this, Jesus had asked His disciples who people thought He was and also who they thought He was. Several answers are given—but God's answer to Jesus' question is not revealed until the Transfiguration. His statement is a combination of phrases from the Law (Moses), the Prophets (Isaiah) and the sacred writings (Psalms). In addition, there are three witnesses to the Father's words, reflecting this same threefold division of Law, Prophets and sacred writings: Moses, Elijah and the Father Himself.

61   See Endnote 55 above; also Chapter 6 of *God's Panoply* (pages 150–152) for an analysis of the first seven words of Genesis 1:1, showing additional multiples of 111 which occur in the gematria and also demonstrates that the design repeatedly uses the golden ratio.

62   *Inscribed* in Hebrew is 'rasham', which not unnaturally contains 'shem', *name*.

63   More significant still is the story of Simon the sorcerer in the book of Acts. Simon the sorcerer of Samaria was a believer. The word used to describe his belief ('pisteuo') has the same root as the word to believe in Romans 10:9 NKJV—'*If you confess with your mouth the Lord Jesus and believe in your heart that God has raised Him from the dead, you will be saved.*' Although Simon was a Christian, Peter could say of him: '*You are poisoned by bitterness and bound by iniquity.*' (Acts 8:23 NKJV)

64   See, for example: www.bibleodyssey.org/en/passages/related-articles/decalogue-as-a-moral-code.aspx or *And God Said: How Translations Conceal the Bible's Original Meaning*

65   Daniel 9:2

66   Rosh Hashanah is a modern two-day holiday, celebrating the beginning of a new year, evoking the creation of the world and the dawn of time. A holiday of new beginnings, it fittingly opens ten Days of Awe or High Holy Days, a season of repentance that allows a person to make a new beginning in the eyes of God.

67 http://www.firstthings.com/web-exclusives/2011/10/days-of-awe
RR Reno is the general editor of the Brazos Theological Commentary on the Bible and author of the volume on *Genesis*.
68 They are the same word in Greek.
69 Here's the perplexing story in full. The threshold implications are not particularly clear in this translation:
Meanwhile, Abner son of Ner, the commander of Saul's army, had taken Ish-Bosheth son of Saul and brought him over to Mahanaim. He made him king over Gilead, Ashuri and Jezreel, and also over Ephraim, Benjamin and all Israel.
Ish-Bosheth son of Saul was forty years old when he became king over Israel, and he reigned two years. The house of Judah, however, followed David. The length of time David was king in Hebron over the house of Judah was seven years and six months.
Abner son of Ner, together with the men of Ish-Bosheth son of Saul, left Mahanaim and went to Gibeon. Joab son of Zeruiah and David's men went out and met them at the pool of Gibeon. One group sat down on one side of the pool and one group on the other side.
Then Abner said to Joab, 'Let's have some of the young men get up and fight hand to hand in front of us.' 'All right, let them do it,' Joab said. So they stood up and were counted off—twelve men for Benjamin and Ish-Bosheth son of Saul, and twelve for David. Then each man grabbed his opponent by the head and thrust his dagger into his opponent's side, and they fell down together. So that place in Gibeon was called Helkath Hazzurim.
The battle that day was very fierce, and Abner and the men of Israel were defeated by David's men. The three sons of Zeruiah were there: Joab, Abishai and Asahel.
Now Asahel was as fleet-footed as a wild gazelle. He chased Abner, turning neither to the right nor to the left as he pursued him. Abner looked behind him and asked, 'Is that you, Asahel?' 'It is,' he answered. Then Abner said to him, 'Turn aside to the right or to the left; take on one of the young men and strip him of his weapons.' But Asahel would not stop chasing him. Again Abner warned Asahel, 'Stop chasing me! Why should I strike you down? How could I look your brother Joab in the face?' But Asahel refused to give up the pursuit; so Abner thrust the butt of his spear into Asahel's stomach, and the spear came out through his back. He fell there and died on the spot. And every man stopped when he came to the place where Asahel had fallen and died.
But Joab and Abishai pursued Abner, and as the sun was setting, they came to the hill of Ammah, near Giah on the way to the wasteland of Gibeon. Then the men of Benjamin rallied behind Abner. They formed themselves into a group and took their stand on top of a hill. Abner called out to Joab, 'Must the sword devour forever? Don't you realize that this will end in bitterness? How long before you order your men to stop pursuing their brothers?'
Joab answered, 'As surely as God lives, if you had not spoken, the men would have continued the pursuit of their brothers until morning.' So Joab blew the trumpet, and all the men came to a halt; they no longer pursued Israel, nor did they fight anymore. All that night Abner and his men marched through the Arabah. They

crossed the Jordan, continued through the whole Bithron and came to Mahanaim. Then Joab returned from pursuing Abner and assembled all his men. Besides Asahel, nineteen of David's men were found missing. But David's men had killed three hundred and sixty Benjamites who were with Abner. They took Asahel and buried him in his father's tomb at Bethlehem. Then Joab and his men marched all night and arrived at Hebron by daybreak.
(2 Samuel 2:8–32 NIV)

70 In *God's Pageantry*, the discussion of 'shaq' occurs in Chapter 2 in the section about the threshold covenant between God and Abraham. God gives Isaac—Yitshaq—a name that has 'threshold' embedded within it. Many centuries later 'shaq' occurs in a punning interchange between God and Jeremiah which also has threshold undertones to it.
In *God's Poetry*, however, I point out that Isaac is a rhyme for 'esek', meaning *dispute* or *contention*—and this is an extremely apt for the shape of Isaac's life. It is also a fitting resonance for this story of Abner and Joab at the Pool of Gibeon.

71 Brian Simmons, *John—Eternal Love*, The Passion Translation. Footnote on John 6:70.

72 Yechiel Eckstein, 'Use It Well', *Holy Land Moments Daily Devotional*, 3 August 2015

73 Dream from 8 November, 1999
In the dream I am an ancient being—a man—and I return to my house (ancestral perhaps) where the young caretaker ridicules me. (I have not been to the house in a long, long time and he has come to regard the place as his own). I am leaving and not coming back. I am anxious not to take too much, so the caretaker does not get angry. But I take a set of drawers, beautifully carved and more ancient than history, a relic of the god Bel, and push them out through a high open window. I then take the one thing I came for with me. However, as I'm departing I notice a small pretty folding table high on a picture rail and I think this would be a very useful thing to have with me too.

74 Steven Collins, Latayne C. Scott, *Discovering the City of Sodom: The Fascinating, True Account of the Discovery of the Old Testament's Most Infamous City*, Howard Books 2013

75 According to Chuck Missler, the names of the five kings of the south, including the king of Sodom, were those of major demon gods. Therefore Abram would have been breaking covenant with Melchizedek, *king of righteousness*, and cutting a covenant with a demon god. Would God have given him a new name in this situation? Not a chance.

76 An examination of John chapters 18 and 19—which is about Peter in the house of Caiaphas—shows how many words are related to Cephas or poetically reminiscent of it in that scene. Peter's Greek name (Petros) is mentioned in verses 10, 11, 15, 16 (twice), 18, 25, 26 and 27. Caiphas (basically the same as Cephas, the *threshold stone*) is mentioned in verses 13, 24 and 28. The Passover (referring to the *passing over of the threshold stone*) is mentioned in verses 28 and 39. The garden ('kepos' or 'kepaios' in Greek) is mentioned in verse 1, 26 and 19:41 while the keeper of the garden ('kepouros') is mentioned in verse

1. The palm of the hand ('kaph' in Hebrew, related to Cephas) is mentioned in verse 22 and 19:3. The door ('thuroros') and the servant girl who keeps the door ('paidiske')—two threshold-related terms—are both mentioned in verse 17. Many scholars think that the unnamed disciple who let Peter in was John himself, keeping his name in the background as usual. I don't think this needs to be the case. This scene is a trial of the covenant over the name Petros/Cephas. And that's the entire focus of the story. To introduce the name of any other disciple at this point would have been to dilute that focus, so that in my view is why John was silent about it.

77   A story so mind-bending it should make a trainwreck of every simplistic theological premise we've ever harboured about God. Here are some other examples: Abimelech negotiates with God in a dream (Genesis 20:3-7) and Ananias negotiates with God (Acts 9:10-17). Linked in with this idea of negotiation is the Divine Council and, along with that, the presence of a true prophet within the Council. Ezekiel 13:9 reveals that false prophets are not in the Council of God's people; Isaiah 5:9-10 carries an implication that Isaiah is present in the Divine Court, while Isaiah 6:8-10 has a question and answer sequence that occurs within the Divine Court. The opening of Habakkuk from 1:1-2:20 suggests a Divine Council vision, similar to that of Isaiah 6. Amos 3:7 is explicit, as are Luke 9, Matthew 17 and Mark 9 which all describe the Transfiguration of Jesus. The Divine Council implication of this threshold scene where Jesus is revealed in glory is further indicated by the appointment of seventy (or seventy-two) disciples almost immediately after the event to go out preaching. Seventy is the number of the Council, as evidenced most notably when the seventy elders go with Moses and Aaron to feast with God on the forbidden mountain in Exodus 24.

www.ingramcontent.com/pod-product-compliance
Lightning Source LLC
Chambersburg PA
CBHW021103080526
44587CB00010B/356